GET YOUR COVID-19 VACCINES

GANIHU ONYEBUASHI

CONTENTS

To the memory of the victims of COVID-19, may they rest in peace.

It may be hard to believe, but their suffering is not wasted.

May those families who lost their loved ones share knowledge and resources with those who suffer from the disease; and may we all learn how to live better and stronger lives.

We hope that their suffering gives everyone the strength to live better lives; that they may be remembered fondly rather than with sadness.

We hope that the knowledge that comes from their deaths will help people live a healthier life and that people who love them will do what is best for them. May their lives be honored and remembered positively.

After all, they did what they could to live a better life even in the face of this horrible disease.

Because of them, a vaccine has been developed, despite the fact that only a small number of people were able to survive.

They opened the door for a vaccine, and may their lives be rewarded. Because of them, medical advancements were made to help prevent, treat, and cure COVID-19.

INTRODUCTION

A coronavirus discovered in 2019, SARS-CoV-2 virus has caused a pandemic of respiratory illness, called COVID-19. COVID-19 is spread through the air. This has an incubation period of about two weeks before symptoms manifest.

COVID-19 primarily presents with mild, influenza like symptoms; fever, cough, shortness of breath, general weakness. However some sufferers develop severe pneumonia which can be fatal if not treated early on.

Researchers currently believe that the coronavirus spreads such as through droplets and virus particles that released into the air if an infected individual breathes, talks, sings, laughs, coughs, or sneezes. The virus can also be transmitted through different contaminated objects and surfaces.

The situation today has changed radically because of COVID-19. We are enduring a global pandemic, with widespread lockdowns to prevent disease transmission and further deaths, while small businesses, and the hopes and dreams of their owners, are being crushed underfoot.

Today COVID-19 has spread worldwide, has infected millions of people. In many countries, life has been turned upside down. Children have been separated from their parents, women have been quarantined in their homes. Hospitals have been closed, streets deserted, and businesses shuttered. Many people wear a surgical masks to protect themselves from the deadly droplets that others breathe into the air.

In most countries, COVID-19 is now a notifiable disease with comprehensive containment measures in place. Surveillance has been increased, as has screening both at ports of entry and at internal borders, with people being asked questions about recent travel history and symptoms of infection.

COVID-19 is a global pandemic, and the world is on the brink of an economic collapse. Individuals who have been affected by this horrific sickness continue to die, and this is causing international distrust and even fear of the very countries that are trying to help them. At present there is no cure against COVID-19, other than medical treatment

However, the vaccines that have been developed can be used to lessen the severity of the disease. Much of the world is more concerned about infectious disease containment, rather than the economic crisis that is unfolding.

Different vaccines have been developed and some exported to neighboring countries. The majority of the world's population has been vaccinated against COVID-19. This is why we do not currently see large numbers of people dying from the virus.

The vaccines against COVID-19 are very effective and provide a high degree of protection. However, further research and development is very needed to develop a vaccine that covers all the known strains. Millions of doses have been manufactured and shipped to neighboring countries. These are the countries that are most in need of vaccines, because they have suffered the greatest impact from COVID-19.

Governments in high-risk areas, with support from the WHO, have enforced mass vaccination. The WHO has advised all countries to maintain a rapid response to any outbreaks of COVID-19. The areas that have been quarantined have been closed to the public. All hospitals are being ordered to maintain preparedness, and provide medical care for anyone who may be infected with COVID-19. Emergency drills are being held in hospitals so that the staff are ready for "worst-case" scenarios.

There is a growing concern that this pandemic could lead to a global recession, which will have devastating consequences for everyone. In some effort to help the economy recover from the COVID-19 crisis, the COVID-19 vaccines might be the answer. There are many COVID-19 sufferers who are now able to work again, thanks to the vaccine. The vaccine has come at an opportune time, just as COVID-19 is fading into the past. Economic advantages are being realized by millions of people who have made a full recovery from COVID-19.

The world is now looking forward towards a bright future, supported by COVID-19 vaccines which have brought much needed hope.

1

CORONA VIRUS

EFFECT OF SARS-COV-2 ON EXTRAPULMONARY ORGAN SYSTEMS

The lungs are most commonly affected organ. Extrapulmonary infections are very rare after acute respiratory infection with SARS-CoV-2 virus. However, despite this, fatal cases have been reported.

The principal pathologic findings in severe cases of SARS-CoV-2 infection include atelectasis and mononuclear cell infiltration in the lung parenchyma. Thoracic radiographs may demonstrate bilateral pulmonary infiltrates. The presence of precapillary and capillary vascular lesions and air bronchograms is indicative of severe disease and warrant hospitalization if confirmed.

The next most commonly affected organ is the heart after the lungs. Rupture of the cardiomyocytes results in myocarditis, which is generally diagnosed by echocardiography. Myocarditis can lead to congestive heart failure.

Coagulopathy due to disseminated intravascular coagulation has been seen in severe cases of COVID-19 infection. It is characterized by a hypocoagulable state, a hyperfibrinolytic state, and a fibrinogen deficit.

The lung and kidney are other major sites of extrapulmonary involvement. Pulmonary involvement is characterized by pneumonitis, which can lead to respiratory failure; this is uncommon after becoming infected with SARS-CoV-2. Renal involvement is characterized by acute renal failure, which is very uncommon.

It may be difficult to distinguish extrapulmonary from primary infection due to the similarity in clinical signs and signs on radiologic studies. The presence of extensive bilateral pulmonary infiltrates may indicate the possibility of systemic secondary bacterial infection. However, this is not always the case.

COVID-19 virus infection also results in a number of noncardiac, nonspecific conduction system abnormalities. Other organs may be involved in a variety of nonspecific ways.

Antigenic and functional characterization of human respiratory mucosal IgA and IgG raised against the SARS-Coronavirus S glycoprotein.

Although most information regarding the SARS-CoV-2 virus has been obtained from experimental studies with animal models, some recently described data have recently been published regarding clinical features and bacterial coinfection associated with human infection with this virus.

The majority of the patients infected by SARS-CoV-2 had mild or atypical clinical manifestations and were rapidly treated with antiviral therapy and recovered. However, several patients developed severe disease and died. The infection was also associated with severe bacterial infections, mainly caused by S. pneumoniae serotypes 4 and 9. Thus, the clinical features of respiratory illness characterized by disseminated infection by SARS-CoV-2 are similar to those observed with other human coronaviruses.

We conclude that SARS-CoV-2 is an important cause of severe respiratory illness in humans and should be included in the panel of severe coronaviruses for diagnostic purposes. However, because of the severity of the disease and the need for a rapid diagnostic test, SARS-CoV-2 should be a sentinel for a new viral infection.

The SARS-CoV-2 virus was isolated from patients with severe respiratory illness who contracted severe respiratory illness after traveling to southern China. No common source or mode of transmission could be found. The virus belongs to a group of coronaviruses that were previously only known from animal infections. The most important clinical, histopathologic, and epidemiologic observations are summarized. The epidemiology of SARS-CoV-2 infection was characterized by a seasonal pattern with outbreaks occurring in March and April. The outbreak pattern was similar to that observed with other human coronaviruses.

HISTORY OF CORONAVIRUS

A novel coronavirus outbreak was first documented in Wuhan, Hubei Province, China in December 2019. Coronaviruses typically cause febrile respiratory illness. Yet, the coronavirus discovered in China had a high fatality rate. It's currently uncertain how this outbreak happened, but it might have been the result of cross transmission during family members caring for other sick people.

Experts say SARS-CoV-2 originated in bats. However, it's still uncertain how the patients contracted the coronavirus. There is no evidence for direct contact between the patients and animals. It's also uncertain whether this virus can be transmitted from person to person.

The first patient was a 68-year-old woman from Jiang'an district. She presented with high fever, cough, shortness of breath and nausea on December 5th, 2019. This female patient had a history of hypertension, hyperlipidemia and coronary heart disease. She was hospitalized in Jiang'an District Central Hospital on December 10th, due to her worsening condition. The woman was diagnosed with pneumonia and transferred to the critical care unit. The patient died on December 13th at 2:30PM after suddenly falling into an irreversible coma.

A health care worker from Jiang'an District Hawashi Hospital notified the Guangzhou Center for Disease Control and Prevention about this outbreak on December 18th, 2019. After an investigation, the first patient was confirmed to have contracted a novel coronavirus. By this time, two more cases had been reported in Jiang'an District (5 people total).

The second patient had a history of chronic renal failure and had recently undergone dialysis treatment before contracting the virus. The third patient was a previously healthy 9-year old girl from Jiang'an District. The girl presented with high fever, cough, shortness of breath and fatigue. The patient reported selling food to patients at Jiang'an District Central Hospital; she may have come in contact with the virus at the hospital.

The World Health Organization (WHO) and Chinese government began to monitor the situation on December 28th. WHO had issued a travel advisory for China on January 5th, asking travelers to avoid unnecessary travel to Wuhan and surrounding areas. The WHO also suggested that patients who had close contact with the first patient should be monitored until the outbreak was over.

The WHO and Ministry of Health of the People's Republic of China (MOH) also called for a mass notification and health education campaign in order to prevent any similar outbreaks.

An emergency meeting was organized by WHO on January 21, 2019 to discuss efforts to tackle this outbreak and prepare for future research on the virus. The meeting concluded that rapid communication between hospitals is necessary as well as coordinated intervention among health care workers and officials.

China put in place the following measures to deal with the outbreak:

During the meeting, experts also discussed different measures for preventing outbreaks of SARS-CoV-2.

Experts proposed that more health care workers should be trained to prevent contact with patients at risk. They stressed that hospitals should develop efficient infection screening systems and implement screening procedures for all new admissions.

MOH provided guidelines on infection control after detecting the virus in Jiang'an District Wuhan City. The guidelines asked health care workers to be more conscientious about washing their hands before and after every patient contact. They also requested disinfection of all rooms used by new patients and cleaning of ward equipment on a regular basis.

On January 23rd, the Chinese Center for Disease Control and Prevention (CDCD) began to implement measures to prepare for future mitigation of this virus. A laboratory was established in Jiang'an District Wuhan City and a team was formed for further research on the virus. The Ministry of Health and CDCD also emphasized that they were working around-the-clock to establish a local epidemic response system in order to quickly prevent more infections.

On January 29th, the WHO officially declared Wuhan City to be in an "increased alert" status. The WHO believed that more patients might be diagnosed with the coronavirus, and they recommended that travelers avoid unnecessary travel to the cities of Wuhan, Hengyang and Gongyi.

On January 31st, Jiang'an District authority held an emergency committee meeting to discuss future steps for dealing with this outbreak. The committee approved a plan that called for greater awareness of Chinese public health officials, industry professionals and local government officials to prevent further spread of Coronavirus.

THE COVID-19 PANDEMIC IN THE WORLD

When the COVID-19 pandemic was first introduced to the world, the first case of infection was met with extreme hostility. On March 13, 2020, President Donald Trump declared a national emergency to combat the spread of COVID-19 in the USA. The next day the European Union, Iran, and North Korea joined in on response. The Ministry of Health announced that they would start to take more extreme steps of containment to prevent the spread of the pandemic. The Ministry of Health would place national health care on lockdown while the military was placed on war footing to launch offensive operations in places infected with COVID-19. The second day that it started, the European Union would introduce new laws allowing for forced euthanasia of individuals with COVID-19. A day later, the Supreme Court ruled against releasing information about COVID-19 to the public stating that they did not want to cause panic.

From the beginning, the Ministry of Health was concerned about the lack of knowledge surrounding the pathogen. Five days after it had been identified, they were still unsure of its effects on individuals infected. They did not have any good information on what would happen if someone got bit or could be infected by contaminated materials. They also did not have any information on how to prevent infection or how to identify infected individuals. They also did not have any information on how to kill the virus in an infected human. The only information they had that time was that there was a high probability of death within 24 hours of infection.

The Ministry of Health's initial response to COVID-19 was to immediately quarantine anyone who showed any signs of infection. Within the first month, 895 cases where identified. The goal was to track these individuals in hopes that they would lead them to a primary vector or sources of infection that could be used against the pandemic. Due to the lack of information and resources, they would not be able to do this. They did, however, identify some of the primary vectors and infected individuals.

It was later discovered that all of the cases that had been identified were only a portion of the actual population infected with COVID-19. The Ministry of Health estimated that there were millions more individuals in the world infected with COVID-19. All of these individuals were being treated in the same way, to the point where it was nearly impossible to track them. The Ministry of Health also could not access these individuals for research because they had all been placed in quarantine facilities. The only way they could access this information was through automatic surveys that were given to them periodically. They would be given a survey that would track their physical, mental, and social health. These surveys took place approximately every two weeks for each infected individual. Using these surveys, the Ministry of Health was able to develop an understanding of how COVID-19 was progressing in infection.

After initializing the screening and containment of individuals infected with COVID-19, a normal grip was placed on the world. Dozens of countries would form their own Ministries of Health and began issuing regulations for various aspects of society. The regulations would range from all aspects of business to what type of clothing people could wear.

STRUCTURE AND CLASSIFICATION

Coronaviruses belongs to the subfamily Coronavirinae in the family of Coronaviridae and the subfamily contains four genera: Alphacoronavirus, Betacoronavirus, Gammacoronavirus, and Deltacoronavirus. CoVs are enveloped viruses with rod-shaped geometries ranging in length from about 30 to 40 nm. The coronavirus particle contains two identical RNA genomes that are folded into separate nucleocapsids, each of which has six coat proteins (three spike or S proteins and three envelope or E2 proteins). The two nucleocapsids are connected at the base by the nucleoprotein, which is connected to the viral envelope by the spike trimer. The nucleocapsids are positive-stranded RNA viruses arranged in a helical symmetry with each strand containing six genes.

The two genomes encode two viral (M (1 capsid protein) and M (2 spike protein)) and two cellular (Protease, Nucleocapsid, Gag, and P RNA), proteins enzymes. The M protease cleaves the precursor Gag-Pol polyprotein into three products: the nucleocapsid, the matrix, and the viral polymerase. The N protein is an RNA-dependent RNA polymerase that assists in replication of the viral genome by catalyzing the synthesis of positive-stranded RNA. The P protein functions during budding of new particles from infected cells.

SARS-CoV 2 contains four structural proteins (S, E, M, and N) and sixteen non-structural proteins (nsp1–16). The genome is made of a single molecule of positive-sense, single-stranded RNA 15,769 nucleotides in length and encodes a SARS-CoV specific protein. There are eleven open reading frames (ORFs) in the genome. ORF 1 to 2 encode two proteins that are related to other coronavirus M proteins, which are involved in cleaving Gag-Pol polyprotein into mature structural and nonstructural proteins during virus assembly. The nsp3 gene encodes the viral spike protein. ORF 3 encodes a small nonstructural protein (nsP3), ORF 4 encodes the viral polymerase (NS5), and ORF 5 encodes a small nucleocapsid protein (nsP1). ORF 6 is involved in virion assembly and has no known function; it contains an internal ribosome entry site (IRES) that serves as a start site for translation of all other proteins. The final seven genes encode proteins that are involved in the regulation of viral replication. The genome is circular, with the largest marker present on one strand, but contains sequence variations on both strands, creating two molecules of viral RNA.

The SARS-CoV-2 spike protein is expressed as multiple conformations which are localized to the plasma membrane and act as receptors for accessory cellular proteins involved in viral entry into cells. The spike protein is located on both RNA molecules and accounts for about 10% of their combined sequence. The spike protein is involved in mediating virion attachment to host cell receptors.

The Origin and Evolution of SARS-CoV-2

The genome sequence of the said coronavirus was compared to other known coronaviruses to determine if it was a unique coronavirus or related to any previously identified virus. The new coronavirus was found to be related to two known viruses, but not more closely related than the lineage I CoVs. The SARS-CoV-2 genome contains numerous mutations, many of which are unique and are likely to have arisen through mutation after the divergence of lineage II CoVs from their common ancestor with lineage I CoVs. No recombination sites were observed in the SARS-CoV-2 genome, which indicates that it is a unique coronavirus. The genome of SARS-CoV 2 has undergone mutations in each of its seven internal ribosomal entry sites (IRES). Because IRESes are located at several places on the viral genome, they are essential for viral replication and infection of new host cells; they act as docking sites for short peptides that initiate translation. The mutations in the IRESes of SARS-CoV 2 have a similar genetic structure to those observed in other CoVs. These changes may be the result of a reaction with a viral protein environment, which further contributes to the evolution of SARS-CoV-2.

The CoVs are enveloped, positive-sense, single-stranded RNA viruses that usually cause acute respiratory disease in humans. CoVs are genetically diverse, with more than 30 strains recognized in 6 species. Genome Evolution of SARS-CoV-2 indicates that the lineage I CoVs are closely related to bat CoVs, whereas the lineage II is more distantly related. The SARS-CoV-2 genome has acquired tens of mutations since its divergence from bats, which indicates that it does not have an ancestral bat CoV. The most recent common ancestor of SARS-CoV-2 evolved around 500 years ago. In contrast, bats have been evolving for millions of years. Therefore, the close relationship between SARS-CoV-2 and lineage I CoVs indicates that those viruses do not have a common ancestor and that they had evolved independently from bats.

SARS-CoV-2 is a zoonotic coronavirus and is related to other coronaviruses that infect bats. The SARS-CoV-2 genome contains 2,000 mutations; 800 of those changes are unique and represent local adaptations to the human host. Twenty-one amino acid substitutions in the spike (S) protein change the receptor binding properties. The mutations in the spike protein resulted in interaction with a different cellular receptor during infection of humans than it did in bats.

Coronaviruses are common causes of low-pathogenicity respiratory tract infections in animals and humans. Humans are becoming more susceptible to infection with coronaviruses, which were once considered to be nonpathogenic viruses. The new coronavirus has a large genome and a high mutation rate which makes it less pathogenic. It is very infectious among young, healthy humans who have not been exposed to other coronaviruses. The new coronavirus can cause severe, debilitating respiratory disease characterized by fever, cough, and shortness of breath. The virus causes severe pneumonia and produces "bronchiolitis" (inflammation of the smallest airways in the lung). It is difficult to distinguish the new disease from the SARS coronavirus. The study shows that humans have had one or more recent cross-species transmission events with a bat coronavirus.

The study clarifies the evolutionary relationships of coronaviruses. The first case of SARS-CoV-2 infection was reported in 2012. It is still unsure whether the new strain is replacing or will replace other strains. There are some regions that are experiencing epidemics of severe acute respiratory syndrome (SARS), which are related to SARS-CoV-2 strains. The study findings open up new research areas on how bats control novel coronavirus infections within their populations and how new strains emerge and spread from bats to humans. Studies of the SARS-CoV-2 genome indicate that the virus is remarkably well adapted to humans. The study has provided valuable information about bats, which could give scientists clues about how to prevent the emergence of new coronaviruses and other infectious diseases.

HOW IS A CORONAVIRUS SPREAD?

Many people have no symptoms at all when they are infected with this virus. However, other people may have fever, cough, fatigue, nausea or diarrhea for one or two weeks before recovering without any long-term effects on their health. It is during the recovery period that healthy people are most infectious. People with severe illness may spread the virus to others by coughing, sneezing or by touching surfaces that have become contaminated with mucus. The virus can remain for several hours on surfaces like doorknobs, spoons and the bottoms of glasses. It is usually spread by shaking hands or touching contaminated objects that are then shared by many people.

If an infected person does not recover, they can still infect others. Most people who do not recover continue to be contagious weeks or months after their illness begins. Those who become very ill may develop severe pneumonia that requires hospitalization. Hospital patients are especially vulnerable to infection because they are exposed to many other people. Therefore, if you are in the hospital, take precautions to limit the spread of germs. At home, limit the number of people who come into the room while you are ill. Also, use separate towels to dry your hands after touching contaminated surfaces. Better isolate people with symptoms of respiratory illness like cough or sore throat. It may also be possible to spread the infection to others when you cough or sneeze. In this case, it is possible to spread the germs in droplets from your nose or mouth.

You can better prevent yourself and others from this illness by washing your hands frequently with soap and water, especially when in close contact with other people, and try to avoid touching your eyes, nose and mouth. This illness is usually mild, but some people develop severe symptoms. Those who are infected with this virus are contagious two weeks before symptoms begin and for four weeks after symptoms disappear. Usually, most people with the virus recover from the infection without treatment. You can help your body by drinking plenty of fluids and getting enough rest.

Although most people recover eventually, some develop severe illness and may need hospitalization.

WHO IS AT RISK FOR INFECTION?

Anyone can get sick with this virus if they are exposed to it. The virus can infect people of all ages and genders, but people who make frequent contact with the public are more likely to get sick. People in close contact with infected people, such as nursing home staff or their family members, are at highest risk of infection. People who travel or live in, or have traveled or lived in, an area where the virus is common are also at risk.

The senior population is considered to be the most vulnerable to the infections transmitted by this virus because of their age and their weakened immune systems. They account for a large number of hospitalizations and deaths from this virus, but all ages are susceptible.

This virus can infect people, especially children, who are severely ill or undernourished. The immune systems of these persons are impaired, leaving them more susceptible to infection. The rate of infection increases significantly when the person becomes very ill (e.g., has an acute febrile illness like pneumonia or flu).

Men or women, especially among those with other conditions that weaken their immune system, are also at higher risk for this disease. Persons with pre-existing medical conditions like diabetes, cancer, hypertension, and lung disease are considered to be at the biggest risk of developing severe symptoms as a result of this virus.

For the general public, the likelihood of having this disease is low, but there are some people who are at higher risk. Of those who were exposed, roughly 1% to 10% of infected individuals will develop severe symptoms; for patients with immunosuppression, this number reaches 20%.

This virus has been found in multiple regions of the world, especially in areas where people live in crowded spaces. It is widespread in communities with high poverty levels.

2

IMPACT OF COVID-19

The presence of COVID-19 has had an enormous impact, not only on the health care system, but also on the economy. The impact has been experienced not only by the countries in which the pandemic broke out, but also by countries that were only potential hosts.

It is important to note that COVID-19 is not just another virus, it is a virus with massive capacity for social and economic disruption. The virus has the capability to destroy entire countries, causing severe nationwide disruptions. It has the ability to devastate economies, causing severe impacts on the standard of living. The virus is capable of creating an exchange rate collapse caused by widespread inflation. COVID-19 is capable of causing mass starvation, creating a situation where thousands are dying every day. All of these effects are wholly possible because COVID-19 disease can be deadly without also inducing fatal symptoms. The virus acts as an amplification factor for poor health conditions. It puts a huge strain on social institutions, requiring massive government intervention to stabilize the situation.

The COVID-19 pandemic shows how incredibly fragile economies can be. The countries most affected by this pandemic were the same countries that were most affected by the global economic recession, including many southern European countries as well as Russia and China. For every COVID-19 case, the country in which it occurs loses approximately 5% of its GDP. This is a trend that begins with the pandemic, but becomes most prominent when the virus is fully spread. Although this has not yet happened in most countries, it is possible for it to happen at any time.

Many people lost their jobs to the increasing demands for their services. Many people also saw their income drop drastically to the point where they were unable to afford basic needs. At its worst, COVID-19 was estimated to have caused a 9% drop in global purchasing power in the year. This drop in purchasing power was enough to cause widespread starvation, which has been shown by past pandemics.

The economic impacts that are not directly tied to direct loss of jobs are much more severe. The international financial markets were adversely affected by the spread of the virus. This has caused huge economic losses in many countries, and is a direct result of COVID-19. In order to stabilize the economy, interest rates were increased in many countries. Bonds and other financial instruments were also sold in attempt to stabilize the markets. In many cases, this was not enough to stop a very high degree of inflation, particularly when a major pandemic occurred. This recession had a significant effect on overall global economic output.

HOW DID THE COVID-19 AFFECT THE ECONOMY

The unprecedented economic damage caused by COVID-19 has forced the United States, one of the most stable economies in the world, into a state of emergency. The government has put additional money into emergency funds and taken over industries such as transportation, tourism and healthcare. The president also approved a $1 trillion funding package for infrastructure development and defense spending.

The global economic recession has also had a negative impact on the U.S. economy due to the increasing number of businesses that have closed down or gone bankrupt, this caused millions of people to lose their jobs or at least their income.

The Stock Market has plummeted in the wake of COVID-19. Due to increased uncertainty regarding the future health of the economy, consumers are more reluctant to spend money on stocks resulting in a negative reaction from investors. The stock market has seen a number of ups and downs since its launch in 2015, but it has never witnessed such a sudden and devastating crash as that which occurred on 2020.

As more money is spent on fighting COVID-19, the U.S. economy's effect on the global economy increases significantly. The United States is such a significant player in the global economy that any changes to its status would significantly affect all other countries.

The trend has been especially noticeable in the South American markets, particularly Brazil and Argentina, where economic policies heavily rely on foreign investment from the United States. As a result of this strong connection between these countries and the United States, when consumer spending in America decreases so does consumer spending in South America.

U.S. companies are also becoming increasingly concerned with the effects of COVID-19 on their businesses. Many companies have already closed down due to economic reasons, but also because they were unable to cope with the effects of COVID-19.

The outbreak of COVID-19 has not only affected the economy in the United States, but worldwide as well. The U.S. economy is such a large part of the global economy that its actions and policies heavily affect those of other countries.

Global leaders commit further support to the US to combat COVID-19

The UN has voted to fully support the United States in their efforts to contain and eliminate COVID-19. The General Assembly of the U. N. supported this resolution unanimously.

Global leaders are in participation at the Global COVID-19 Summit hosted by the United States has affirmed its commitment to ensuring equitable access to COVID-19 vaccines for all countries through COVAX – noting that equitable access is so important to end the acute stage of the pandemic.

Global leaders and representatives from the governments of Canada, the European Union, France, Germany, Italy and the United Kingdom met recently in New York to find solutions to COVID-19.

The United States has outlined a multi-pronged approach to help contain and eliminate COVID-19. The plan seeks to reduce or eliminate the spread of the virus by or before 2025, and supports efforts to develop a vaccine that could be used across the world. In addition, the United States is working with other governments and civil society leaders to expand access to life-saving antiviral medicines for those who are at risk from COVID-19 infection.

IMPACT OF COVID-19 ON PEOPLE'S LIVELIHOODS, HEALTH AND OUR FOOD SYSTEMS

Since the very start of the pandemic there has been a shortage of meat, dairy and vegetables. Border closures, trade restrictions and the confinement measures have been preventing farmers from accessing the markets, including for buying the inputs and selling their produce, and agricultural workers from harvesting crops, thus destroying domestic and also international food supply chains and reducing access to healthy, safe and diverse diets. Due to the closure of borders and markets, export and import of animals and animal products is prohibited and regulated. Livestock traders have been unable to move animals between countries or trading zones, especially from/to areas designated as

Level 4 – High Risk – or where isolation and border control measures are in place.

Controls imposed on the movement of animals, animal-derived products and foodstuffs have had widespread implications for people's livelihoods at all levels of the food system.

Maintaining livestock is an important element of household economies. It provides an important source of income, manure to fertilize crops and feed, meat for household consumption and other benefits including social status. As a consequence of heightened border controls, movement restrictions have affected livestock traders in countries affected by the disease.

The lack of income from sales of animals and animal products has had important implications for livelihoods.

As access to markets has been restricted, traders have experienced financial losses due to the inability to sell telemetered animals (cattle, sheep and goats), among others.

They have also had to meet additional costs associated with making necessary changes to improve animal welfare (e.g. in pig and poultry farming).

Some of these changes include:

The outbreak of disease has had direct impact on producers and their communities, who have been unable to get access to markets for selling their animals and animal products. This has led to economic hardship for producers, without any means of generating alternative income.

As breadwinners lose their jobs, fall ill and die, the food security and millions of women and men's nutrition are jeopardized, particularly in low-income countries, especially the most marginalized populations that include the small-scale farmers and indigenous peoples, being hardest hit. These families and communities cannot afford to buy food or pay for transport, risk losing their livelihoods and struggle to make ends meet.

Millions of agricultural workers have been affected by border closures, movement restrictions and the outbreak of the disease.

Loss of income for recreational animal keepers, in both rural and urban areas, has a significant impact on livelihoods in both developed and developing countries.

As a result of the loss in income, many people have been forced to reduce their spending on food. In areas already affected by food insecurity this could lead to a worsening of conditions.

People in border areas are suffering from food insecurity, as they are unable to buy food, especially staple crops. Their ability to earn an income has diminished making it difficult for them to buy goods. The lack of income generation has led to hunger, malnutrition and family separation as women leave their children with relatives or inexperienced caregivers in order to find paid employment.

In areas with limited livelihood mobility restrictions on movement of animals, animal products and foodstuffs have resulted in the disruption of domestic and international food supply chains. The resulting price increases, especially for staples such as rice, maize, wheat and vegetable oils has extended the gap between rich and poor in many countries.

THE IMPACT OF COVID-19 ON EDUCATION

The global lockdown of education institutions in the past year has affected schools, universities, and institutions of all sorts. Many institutions of learning and classrooms have been closed and their pupils and staff have been affected. COVID-19 has many direct and indirect effects on the education process. These effects are in the form of restrictions, closures, and all other things to do with education.

Specifically, some of these effects of COVID-19 include a decrease in school attendance and a decrease in the number of students that actually enroll at institutions of learning. Many teaching staff have been laid off as a result of the shutdown of their institutions, and as a result, educational quality has suffered. Most importantly, the future generation is going to be deprived of an education. This would have a negative effect on many things ranging from the country's economy to its stability and even its security.

With the advent and the popularity of virtual learning and distance learning platforms such as internet and email, is the only way for the country to cope with this kind of problem in our society. The use of these platforms should be encouraged in our educational system. Any courses that cannot be taught via the web, such as sports or physical activities must be cut off for the time being and saved for later when the situation has become more stable.

Moreover, studying abroad is no longer an option for many students due to COVID-19. It was one of the most popular options for students to get an education in some Western countries, especially in America. Other countries are also not an option since they are sometimes considered to be too dangerous. This has led many students to lose hope on pursuing higher education.

However being vaccinated will prevent further negative effects on the country. By giving this vaccine to many people, we will be able to reduce the negative effect of COVID-19 on our society. This vaccine will ensure that our future generation is well-educated and has a bright future ahead of them.

Overall, I believe that COVID-19 is affecting education in a negative way since most students these days especially those who are about to complete their secondary education are scared to continue with their education due to the closure of schools and institutions and the high rate of death caused by this Covid-19 virus.

IMPACT OF COVID-19 ON TOURISM

The impact of COVID-19 on tourism has been devastating. Hotels were left completely empty for extended periods of time, restaurants had fewer customers, and the loss in tourism revenue is estimated to be in the billions.

Before COVID-19, travel and tourism had become one of the most important sectors in the world economy, generating a total of $7 trillion in sales worldwide. This is more than the entire world's oil market worth. In

2015, it is estimated that travel and tourism contributed to almost 10 per cent of global gross domestic product (GDP).

Travel and tourism continued to grow around the world due to improved roads, lower prices of air tickets, more developed transportation networks, increasing urbanization, increasing demands by the developing countries for modernization, stability and security in their own countries.

After COVID-19, tourist visits plummeted worldwide. In the United States, the Global Tourism Monitoring Program reported a 37 per cent drop in international tourist arrivals. International tourism also suffered at a time when the U.S. needed to increase tourism if it wanted to reduce unemployment and stimulate its economy.

In response to the COVID-19 virus, many countries closed their borders to foreign travelers. The United States President Donald Trump even issued an executive order banning imports of goods produced outside the country and closed all land, sea and air borders. This is the only time in recent history that borders were completely shut and no country was allowed entrance or exit.

The United States economy which is considered as the world's largest economy, was devastated by COVID-19. The United States also suffered from what many economists call the "coastalization" effect. This means that those people living in coastal areas became more dependent on tourism for their livelihoods.

The impact of COVID-19 on the world economy extended beyond tourism to all sectors of the national economies. Many scientists believe that COVID-19 is one of the most serious threats to our global economy.

PRESERVING THE PLANET -- MITIGATING IMPACTS ON NATURE AND CULTURE

The sudden fall in tourism cuts off funding for biodiversity conservation. Some 7% of world tourism relates to wildlife, a segment growing by 3% annually. Conservationists worldwide are one of the most affected by COVID-19.

One such group, the International Union for Conservation of Nature (IUCN) works to ensure that nature is conserved and sustainably used. It supports scientific analysis and policy recommendations on crucial issues such as climate change, biodiversity, and sustainable development.

IUCN took a hard hit from COVID-19 and has struggled to adapt and raise money since the onset of the virus. The IUCN's financial backing from governments is greatly reduced and the funding gap is estimated to have been between $2m and $5m a year.

IUCN will have to find alternative sources of funding if it is to continue its work.

Most of the major wildlife charities also lost a significant amount of money through COVID-19, including the World Wildlife Fund, Save the Elephants, the African Wildlife Foundation and World Wide Fund for Nature. The recent closure of borders deprived these organizations of a valuable source of revenue.

In addition, the loss of tourists from the United States and Europe has been a crippling effect on the tourism industry and part of this has been compensated by the explosion of interest generated by China and India.

Loss of revenue is also a serious concern for many organizations involved in education. Many global education programs rely heavily on the revenues generated from foreign students. Most were able to withstand COVID-19 until recently but with tourism taking such a huge hit they are now facing drastic cuts in their budgets.

Citizens, nonprofit organizations, schools and universities can all be affected by COVID-19. As the crisis continues, the risk of it jumping to new areas increases. While not all schools and universities will be affected, because of the potential for COVID-19 to spread across the world there is a significant risk that it could.

The United States government took emergency measures to help its universities and others cover the loss in funds caused by COVID-19. Although there were no direct funding cuts to any university or organization, certain programs throughout the country have seen reductions in their budget which are likely to increase in future years.

COVID-19 also had a significant effect on the museum industry. A large number of museums and collections were affected by the viral outbreak and many had to close their doors. Many museums had to carry out emergency measures in order to prevent the loss of valuable artifacts due to COVID-19.

Although many of these impacts have been felt worldwide, some have been more drastic than others. In areas such as Africa, tourism is so important that closures have left entire communities completely destitute.

The U.S. government has spent trillion of dollars trying to contain the virus. The United States government has invested over $50 billion in developing vaccines, drugs and surveillance to fight COVID-19.

The response to COVID-19 by the U.S. government was unprecedented. There are currently four different bioweapons laboratories around the world actively researching COVID-19 in their efforts to find a cure for the virus.

In addition to the four bioweapons labs, the U.S. government has spent over a trillion dollars over the last 2 years on a variety of other countermeasures, including a nationwide border control system and a program to isolate potential infected areas, as well as programs to increase coverage for mass vaccination .

The Center for Disease Control and Prevention is also actively researching ways to prevent further outbreaks of COVID-19. In 2020, they began testing vaccines against the virus which has proved to be successful. They are hoping to find a cure for COVID-19 by 2025.

3

SYMPTOMS OF COVID-19?

Symptoms differ from person to person. The virus affects people in different ways. A large number of infected persons will develop mild to moderate symptoms, and will even recover without being admitted to the hospital. On the other hand, others will develop severe symptoms and require treatment in an intensive care unit (ICU). The severity of symptoms will greatly vary according to one's individual response to the virus. The severity level (HL) is an indicator that explains how well a person is responding to treatment for COVID-19.

Most common symptoms:

Fatigue

The body feels tired even when the person is at rest.

Sore throat

Intense soreness in one's throat is another common symptom associated with this disease. For some, the sore throat is accompanied by fever.

Fever

A sudden high fever over 39 degrees Celsius is a moderate symptom of the disease. The body will feel hot even when ambient temperatures are low. Fever, especially when it occurs in combination with other symptoms, can make a person feel very uncomfortable and weak.

Sneezing and coughing

When a person is infected with this disease, it is very likely that they will begin to sneeze and cough frequently. If someone is infected with this virus, it is very likely that they will begin to sneeze and cough frequently.

Loss of taste or smell

In some cases, an affected person may lose their sense of taste or smell. In these cases, food may not taste as tasty as before, and the person may find it difficult to enjoy the flavor of the food because of their poor sense of smell or taste.

Less common symptoms:

Headache

The virus affects the brain. If the neurologic system is affected, it can result in headaches. The degree of severity would depend on how severe the virus is affecting the brain. The degree of severity also depends on one's age and health status, plus how long it has been since infection. The longer that you have been exposed to the virus, the less severe your symptoms will be.

Nausea

Nausea is another common symptom that is associated with this disease. Most people will experience some level of nausea. The severity of nausea varies according to how severe the virus has spread. If someone is infected with this virus, it is very likely that they will feel nauseous. When one's disease progresses, it can result in vomiting.

Diarrhea and abdominal pain

Another symptom commonly associated with this disease is diarrhea. The virus can be extremely painful, especially when it begins to spread into the colon.

Physical exhaustion

If this disease progresses, physical fatigue can develop. This is because the COVID-19 virus steals our energy by metabolizing our muscles. Muscles become tired easily and strain easily during exertion. When one has COVID-19, they can experience soreness in their limbs. There is a good reason for this; the disease makes muscles weaker, which means that it will be physically exhausting to move about.

Rash on skin, or discoloration of fingers or toes

The COVID-19 virus is a contagious virus. That means that it can spread through direct contact with bodily fluids or from an infected person. In severe cases, the virus could cause a rash to develop on the skin, or discoloration of fingers or toes. A rash will vary in color from light to dark in different people.

Red or irritated eyes

Sometimes, an infected person's eyes will become red or irritated.

Serious symptoms:

Difficulty breathing or shortness of breath

Some people with COVID-19 will begin to have difficulty breathing. Shortness of breath can also develop if the virus has spread into the lungs. Some people will experience this symptom because of heart failure. Because of this, respiration will be affected, making many types of activity very difficult, including sleep. As one's disease progresses, breathing can become more difficult.

Loss of speech or mobility, or confusion

In most cases, if a virus affects the brain, they can begin to lose their speech. In some cases, the person will not be able to move or feed themselves. This is very dangerous.

Chest pain

If COVID-19 has spread into the lungs, it can result in chest pain. This symptom will be highly correlated to heart failure. If the heart is not really functioning properly, then it will be difficult for your body to circulate blood around your body. Because of this, you may feel pain in your chest.

The treatment for this disease depends largely on the severity of symptoms. When a person has mild or moderate symptoms it may be better to treat his or her condition at home with rest and fluids rather than being admitted to a hospital. In severe cases where blood pressure is low, it may be necessary to call 911 for emergency medical help.

Infected persons may have difficulty feeling some of the symptoms because the virus is so active. Generally a person's immune system will react quickly to control the infection. This causes a person to recover on its own. In some cases, taking medicine will be necessary to help a person recover.

Many people who have been diagnosed with COVID-19 will recover without any problems. Others who are usually healthy will still feel weak and fatigued after the symptoms subside for between one to two weeks. In general, COVID-19 infection is not life-threatening. If a person is diagnosed with the virus, they should be monitored as recommended by their doctor.

The treatment for COVID-19 is effective. However, the treatment for this virus varies depending on the individual. For some people, treatment may not be necessary. It is recommended that individuals with this condition drink plenty of fluids and rest as much as possible during recovery. In some cases, doctors may also want to give a person drugs to help speed up their recovery from this infection.

The virus causes a mild cold and affects the respiratory system, sometimes causing shortness of breath or trouble breathing. If people have symptoms, they should call their doctor right away. This case might be difficult to treat.

COVID-19 can affect your immune system, causing signs and symptoms that may result in death. If the infection continues to spread through your body, there is no cure. If this infection spreads, many viruses will begin to attack the brain and other vital organs of the body, causing death.

WHY THE LUNGS ARE PARTICULARLY AFFECTED?

Some germs can enter the lungs. Therefore, the immune system is put under great pressure to fight against infection. Under these circumstances, it is very useful for immune cells to have extra energy. That's why the body produces more white blood cells in order to properly protect our body against infection. We need them all the time not only for this single battle but also for many other battles during our life time. That is why the immune system has an extra amount of white blood cells in our lungs. Those white blood cells are the ones that fight infections in the lungs. The reason why they are there is to make sure that they are ready to fight if an infection breaks through anywhere in our body.

Sometimes people think that they have so many different problems, so they don't need vaccinations for all at once. They think that they will have a better immune system if they take the vaccines only once a year.

But what happens after that is that the body starts to forget about vaccinations and adapts to being exposed to many different things it needs to fight for examples for illnesses, without remembering them. This is dangerous for our personal health because an important weapon can never be ready at all times, so it will be useless in time of war.

We have many different ways of protecting our body from being exposed to bacteria or viruses. Some of them are very difficult to remember. Others still can be forgotten by our body very quickly. If we have a long battle against bacteria or viruses, we will need a stronger weapon to secure victory for our army.

After the first dose, the body needs some time to be ready for a fight. When we talk about fighting against bacteria and viruses, we mean fighting against them in our body. That's why we need time to prepare our immune system before we start the battle for infection and illness.

At present, having two doses of vaccines is necessary. This is because of more and more germs around us and more and more people coming from all around the world to stay in our country. This means that we are more likely to be exposed to many new diseases.

I HAVE ASTHMA, WHAT DOES COVID-19 MEAN FOR ME?

COVID-19 means that there is a new form of influenza or flu virus and it's been proven to be worse than regular flu. It is the most severe form of the virus, and it has been confirmed even more deadly than the regular influenza.

If you have an asthma attack triggered by the virus, you will be hospitalized for a prolonged period of time. In severe cases, you will need to be admitted into the ICU.

The viruses are very dangerous for asthmatics and can be fatal if they are ingested within their lungs. So it's a good idea to avoid having any contact with them, and keep your distance from anyone that is coughing or sneezing around you.

Avoid going outside, and keep your distance from flu-like symptoms, because there is a possibility that you might get infected.

If you have an asthma attack triggered by a respiratory virus, a COVID-19 or any other respiratory virus for that matter, your breathing will be compromised. Your breathing will slow down to the point where it will become almost impossible to breathe.

Because your oxygen level is dropping fast, you'll start experiencing some side effects like nausea. You'll also feel like vomiting when the full panic attack kicks in.

Then you will start seeing spots in front of your eyes, and when you try to breathe, you will experience a very strong pain in your chest. You'll probably feel like your heart is about to explode, or that you're going to die right in front of your eyes.

People who have asthma attacks triggered by the lungs and the respiratory viruses will be confined to their bed and will need medical attention. The severe condition will leave them feeling very unwell and weak. They will also need immediate care just in case they lose consciousness at any time.

You should take the necessary precautions in order to avoid getting infected, because once you are infected, it's hard for your body to fight it off. Because of this, it's very important that you manage your condition better if you already have asthma. Visit your doctor and be sure that your asthma is under control; otherwise, you run the risk of having more asthma attacks.

If you are already suffering from asthma, especially if it's triggered by the flu virus, immediately get medical help. Your doctor will give an advice to take a medication to help you fight the flu.

If you have an asthma attack triggered by the flu virus, don't expect any other strain to have a different effect on your condition. The virus that causes your asthma attack will still affect your breathing ability.

You'll need to contact your doctor if you're having severe breathing problems because of this respiratory virus. Because of the progression of the flu, your breathing will deteriorate very quickly.

Asthmatics shouldn't try to overuse their inhalers because they can be very harmful if you use them too often. So always follow your doctor's instructions and never take more than the recommended dosage.

The sufferer of asthma who has a respiratory virus is pretty much delicate. But one thing that you can do to ease the situation is to consult with your doctor and get yourself on some medication to help you fight off the virus.

DEATH RATE CAUSED BY CORONAVIRUS

Covid-19 continues to infect people in the U.S., Europe, and other countries around the world. The spread of the virus also continues to increase in many

Asian regions. Countries in Asia that have been affected by COVID-19 have suffered an economic impact in billions of dollars in the tourism, transportation, and medical service industries.

In August 2021, the average of more than 700 people per day continue to die of COVID-19 in the U.S. This has caused COVID-19 to become one of the deadliest viruses in history, with an estimated 5,000 deaths per week. The side effect of COVID-19 is severe organ failure and the inability of the body's immune system to fight off the virus; it is spreading with little resistance.

The global cases as of August 5, 2021, has 199,803,078 positive result, of which there are 4,251,176 deaths. Given that a large number of cases are asymptomatic, and patients can be properly treated, the estimated number of deaths from Coronavirus is still substantially increasing. As of August, 2021, the rate of the Coronavirus death is 19.3% of all deaths caused by viruses.

Thankfully, countless scientists and doctors are working hard on a vaccine and a cure to COVID-19, but for now, we can help by getting vaccinated against this deadly virus.

The best way to avoid this disease is to get vaccinated as soon as possible.

When you have not already been vaccinated against COVID-19, NOW IS THE TIME! You may be saving your life. The sooner you get the vaccination, the better your chance of avoiding this virus.

With the rapid vaccinations in the months when vaccines first became widely available, COVID-19 deaths have decreased. This is a good sign and shows that everyone is taking the proper precautions and getting vaccinated. The sooner someone gets vaccinated, the more likely they are not to get the virus in the first place.

We really should all take the necessary precautions and get ourselves vaccinated against this disease.

We need to act now because what happens tomorrow may be too late for us to act today.

There are so many vaccines being developed all around the world. The more we work together, the greater our chance of finding a solution to COVID-19. The faster COVID-19 is eliminated from the population, the better this will be for our world.

The data represents the total number of deaths worldwide according to Reuters tally from January 2021 to August 2021 for COVID 19:

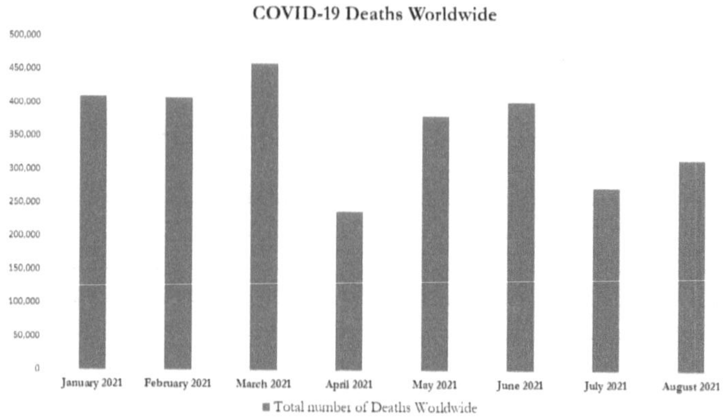

There are 408,980 deaths in January 2021, 406,715 deaths in February 2021, 457,906 in March 2021, 236,885 in April 2021, 380,031 in May 2021, 401,215 in June 2021, 273,869 in July 2021, and 315,058 in August 2021.

4

WHAT IS THE BEST WAY FOR PEOPLE WHO ARE ALREADY EXPOSED TO COVID-19?

If you already exposed to COVID-19 there are some ways you can take to prevent someone or your love ones from getting sick from you.

It is better to isolate yourself to avoid spreading the virus. Take rest and avoid touching or kissing anyone to prevent the virus from spreading.

As much as possible, you should wash your hands with soap and water to avoid infecting others nearby such as family members, friends, co-workers and neighbors.

It is really important that individuals protect themselves and their loved ones by wearing masks even inside their homes until they have been evaluated.

Letting others know about your status can help them protect themselves by taking preventative measures to keep themselves healthy.

When you experience symptoms of COVID-19, please contact your local health department or call the CDC for further guidance.

The US government has collected data on individuals who have had contact with people with COVID-19, but not all of them are confirmed cases. Because of this, it is important that anyone who has had contact with a person with COVID-19 gets evaluated by a doctor right away so they can be taken off the potential high-risk list.

TESTING

The declaration of the COVID-19 pandemic was directly connected to testing regimes that were implemented internationally, mostly following the guidance of the WHO. The predominant test used, particularly in the early stages of the pandemic, was the RT qPCR test (reverse transcription quantitative polymerase chain reaction).

This test uses methods that find fragments of viral RNA in cell samples. After a small amount is processed, depending on the sensitivity of the test, a fragment of viral RNA is amplified in a large quantity by a polymerase chain reaction. The test can give information about whether there is virus present in a sample.

In order to perform this testing regime, the scientific community had to standardize protocols and protocols for assuring everything from proper specimen handling to proper hot-tissue management.

Besides the diagnostic test for COVID-19, other tests were implemented to determine whether a person had been infected and to establish whether those who were suspected of having been infected with the virus should be quarantined. These tests were based on semi-quantitative RT PCR or antigen detection, as well as real-time RT PCR combined with fluorescent antibodies (FNA), as well as FISH (fluorescent in situ hybridization) and digital PCR.

One of the most serious issues that arose during the pandemic was whether a person presented with symptoms was infected, and how to determine this. In addition, what treatment they should receive. In theory, it would be most sensible for a person presenting with symptoms to be quarantined for 21 days, after which only those people who tested negative could be allowed out of quarantine. However, according to guidelines from the WHO, an incubation period of 14 days must be observed before ruling that a person is infected.

During this period, the person must test positive for COVID-19. This raises problems because symptoms can appear at any time within this period, leading to uncertainty about whether the person is infected.

Additionally, a person presenting with symptoms may not be a carrier of the virus. For example, a symptomatic carrier who was symptomatic at the time of their outbreak would have been infected from another source. Over time, the virus would lose its infectivity and thus could not be detected by conventional detection methods. To cope with this difficulty, the WHO has stressed the importance of ruling out alternatives to infection such as other viruses or bacteria before trying to determine whether or not an individual is infected.

Another major issue is that of drug resistance. Because of the simple structure of the virus, the possibility exists that it may be mutated to resist particular treatment options. For example, although Tamiflu has been proven to be effective against COVID-19 in cases where it has been tested, there is still no guarantee that this will hold true during a future pandemic. As a result, many patients who have recovered from COVID-19 have ended up being hospitalized due to complications arising from treatment.

A crucial concern is that the virus may mutate so quickly that it is no longer detectable by conventional methods. For this reason, a new approach using COVID-19 production and testing systems is being researched.

Although there were no cases of mutation, the virus was still able to kill most infected patients. The symptoms that afflicted most victims were an extremely high fever, fatigue and respiratory symptoms. Infection would also often cause the development of nausea, vomiting, diarrhea and abdominal pain. Due to these types of symptoms, it became difficult for infected patients to maintain their daily activities with moderate consequences. At times, patients with COVID-19 exhibited a fatal course.

The testing was meant to provide both a statistical indicator of the spread of the virus and a mechanism for determining whether to implement mass quarantine. From the beginning, the WHO recognized that early detection and identification were an important first step in responding to any outbreak. Thus, surveillance and testing were first and foremost on the WHO's agenda from its earliest deliberations on COVID-19. The most widely used test for COVID-19 was the RT qPCR, which is sufficiently accurate to provide at least a very rough idea of whether or not an individual is infected with the virus. The RT qPCR test determines if there are enough viral particles in the sample to perform extensive amplification. If so, it uses real-time PCR to verify that the amplification has occurred correctly.

The distinction between whether a person is infectious or not is extremely important. Generally, if a person is shedding particles of virus that pose more than a very remote risk of infecting others, they should be quarantined. Although the first indicator of infection is the level of viral shedding, this should not be viewed as a 'correct' test, but rather as an indicator that there may be infection and that the person might still carry the virus.

The need for early detection is also stressed by the WHO. The WHO notes that an early diagnosis will benefit patients by allowing them to avoid complications. Ideally, infection should be detected in large enough numbers of people before the virus becomes resistant to available medications. This would be beneficial to those people's health as well as a preventative measure against the emergence of drug-resistant strains of the virus.

WHO ARE CONSIDERED AS CLOSE CONTACTS IN THE CONTEXT OF COVID-19?

Those who interacted with a person with COVID-19 within one meter for more than 15 minutes during the two weeks prior to the onset of illness.

Considered close contacts include neighbors, coworkers, classmates, doctors and health workers who have been in frequent contact with a person with COVID-19.

The close contacts of a person with COVID-19 will be interviewed on behalf of that person during epidemiological research for disease prevention purposes.

One of the element of contact tracing programs public health experts deem critical to controlling the COVID-19 outbreak includes finding and testing close contacts of known positive cases. This study aims to determine whether close contacts that are exposed to the virus within one meter do acquire clinical symptoms or signs of infection.

If you are a close contact of a person with COVID-19, you must be tested. Testing involves taking a blood sample, getting a swab of mucous membranes, and taking an oral temperature.

You might be asked to provide information about relationships with people who are positive for COVID-19. It is important to tell the people you have known in the last two weeks about any contact you have had with them during this time period. There is no way to predict who will become infected with COVID-19 or who will have symptoms or signs. Once you are a close contact of a person that has symptoms, then you are also at risk for becoming infected with this COVID-19 or developing symptoms.

Exposure to COVID-19 can be as simple as touching a door handle or touching something that another person has touched. It is important to know the people that you have had contact with, and it is also important to let yourself informed about the situation at all times.

Because COVID-19 is so deadly, we need to do everything we can as quickly as possible so we don't get infected and pass the virus onto others.

HOW WILL THE HOME MANAGEMENT OF MILD OR MODERATE SYMPTOMS OF COVID-19?

If you have been in contact with an individual who has COVID-19, you must be prepared to manage mild or moderate symptoms. Because symptoms of COVID-19 manifest in the respiratory tract, the mucous membranes and gastrointestinal tract, it is important to know how to treat mild or moderate symptoms.

If you do start getting symptoms, it is vital that you be able to recognize them and treat yourself at home. There are a few treatments that will ease your symptoms while you wait for antiviral medicine, but it is best if you get professional medical help as soon as possible.

The first step to take is to contact your doctor. A doctor can determine if you have had any signs or symptoms of COVID-19, make sure your fever is not higher than 100 degrees Fahrenheit, and make sure the treatment for your symptoms is suitable for you.

The way home management of mild or moderate symptoms works is that the doctor will dispense medicine to you at home and then call and check in with you within a few hours to see how you are doing. If your symptoms begin to get worse, then the doctor will call and prescribe more medicine to take at home if needed. The doctor can also prescribe medicine for you to take under the care of a medical professional if need be.

If for any reason your symptoms change from mild or moderate, make sure you tell your doctor because any changes will influence their treatments.

Symptoms of COVID-19 include:

1. Mild flu-like symptoms such as fever, cough, and runny nose (an infected person without medical treatment may get a temperature of up to 104 degrees Fahrenheit)
2. Moderate flu-like symptoms such as high temperature (up to 110 degrees Fahrenheit) and difficulty breathing.

COVID-19 kills the cells in the respiratory tract and makes it harder for you to breathe properly. When you have a fever and trouble breathing, it is important to get medical treatment right away because the rate at which the virus kills your cells will increase and you can develop respiratory failure.

Those with moderate symptoms will be encouraged to use cough and cold medicines that are sold over the counter (OTC) for common colds. These medications contain only mild painkillers, expectorants, decongestants and cough suppressants; they may not treat the virus. Medications such as ibuprofen (Advil, Motrin) or acetaminophen (Tylenol Cold or Tylenol Extra Strength) may help with pain and fever, but they can have unwanted side effects that complicate things. These medications may also disrupt the body's ability to fight off the virus.

Moderate symptoms of COVID-19 can last for up to two weeks. During this time, it is crucial to get enough rest and hydration and take over-the-counter medications for common colds. If one needs medical care, they should provide their regular home address and phone number.

Some doctors will not treat mild or moderate symptoms of COVID-19 with any medication. This is because antiviral medicine can develop resistance to the virus over time and it is impossible to know if the medicine will still be effective.

The United States government has collected data on individuals who have had contact with people with COVID-19, but not all of them are confirmed cases. Because of this, it is important that anyone who has had contact with a person with COVID-19 gets evaluated by a doctor right away so they can be taken off the potential high-risk list.

HOW COULD I PROTECT MY FAMILY FROM COVID-19 AT HOME?

It is not easy to stop COVID-19 entirely, but it is possible to keep your home and also your loved ones as safe as possible from the virus.

1. Do not handle the virus. When you have been in contact with a person who has COVID-19, make sure you do not touch them, their belongings, or anything they have touched.
2. Always wear a mask whenever you are in public to avoid spreading the virus.
3. Wash your hands frequently with soap and warm water or use hand sanitizer when you do not have the access to soap and water.
4. Do not use door knobs, light switches, or other surfaces that have been touched by a person who has COVID-19.
5. Do not eat food that has been touched by someone who has COVID-19 and clean up spills immediately.
6. Use tissues with either COVID-19 on them or throw them away in a plastic bag, never in the toilet.
7. Wash your clothes in hot water to clean off any COVID-19 that may be on them.
8. Use disinfectant spray to disinfect surfaces that have been touched by someone who has COVID-19 or are potentially infected.
9. Stay indoors as much as possible, especially if you are sick with mild or moderate symptoms of COVID-19.

10. Avoid sharing items such as cups and plates with anyone who has COVID-19.
11. If you happen to touch a surface that has been touched by someone who has COVID-19 then wash your hands with soap and water immediately afterwards.
12. Wait at least 14 days after your symptoms have subsided to leave your home and visit friends or relatives. This will make sure you do not spread the virus if you do not have it yourself.
13. If you think someone has COVID-19, call your local health department and tell them before your family member or friend notices symptoms. They could send someone over to evaluate the person and make sure they are safe at home or bring them to the hospital.
14. If you notice someone has flu-like symptoms, do not approach them until you are certain they do not have COVID-19.
15. If you know someone with high-risk exposure to COVID-19, make sure to keep your distance from them until you are certain they do not have the virus; some people may want to keep their distance even if they are uninfected. If you have any questions, talk to your doctor.

HOW DO I REMOVE COVID-19 FROM MY HOME?

It is safe to say that you need to take precautions when it comes to removing COVID-19 from your home. Never touch something with your bare hands, and use a disinfectant to sanitize surfaces that COVID-19 has touched. Always use gloves when working with disinfectants and never allow the cleaners to come into contact with your eyes, nose, or mouth.

A common way to remove COVID-19 is to use a steam cleaner. Steam cleaners emit high pressure steam that kills any virus or bacteria on the surface of the item you are cleaning. The best way to remove COVID-19 is to clean with hot water, which is hotter than 100 degrees Fahrenheit.

Clean the following with hot water:

1. Carpets and rugs in your home
2. Clothing, sheets, and blankets in your home.
3. Door handles
4. Light switches in your home
5. Refrigerator handles
6. Sponges and cloths used for cleaning (make sure they are not used by someone who has not been vaccinated)

7. Windows
8. Toilets
9. Wall outlets
10. Water faucet handles
11. Any surface that has come into contact with the virus (stepping on an infected doorknob, for example)
12. Do not clean with bleach or abrasive chemicals. These will contribute to the spread of the infection and your home will just become dirtier if you use these harsh cleaners on surfaces with COVID-19 on them.

THERE IS NO ANTIVIRAL TO TREAT COVID-19. WHAT IS THE APPROACH TO TREATMENT?

The person who has symptoms should be seen by a health care provider. They may have to take some medication under a doctor's supervision. If they are told they need to take medication, it means they will need to stay in the hospital or longer for observation. They may need medication that targets COVID-19, such as acyclovir, or one that helps them to tolerate medications.

They may need fluids and pain relief. Depending greatly on how severe their symptoms are, they may require oxygen.

Heating pads and humidifiers may be used to lessen congestion and improve comfort during the time of illness; heating pads can also help alleviate pain associated with fever. This is not a substitute for traditional treatment by a doctor or emergency department of a hospital setting.

HOW MANY PEOPLE HAVE SYMPTOMS THAT ARE LIKELY TO CAUSE SEVERE ILLNESS?

The people who have signs but no symptoms, about one in five will develop severe illness. The severity of the illness will be mild or moderate in most cases, but it can be life-threatening, and may require hospitalization. Those who have difficulty breathing may require oxygen. People with severe illness will be treated as soon as they are seen. Many of these people require oxygen to breathe. To provide oxygen for many people, a special way of making oxygen will be needed. The people with signs and symptoms have a greater chance of having severe illness. They should be treated in the hospital.

5

HOW TO PREVENT THE PRESENCE OF COVID-19 IN YOUR BODY?

As you know, COVID-19 is an infectious disease that can be transmitted by air or water. It's also possible for this virus to be transmitted via touching contaminated objects which already contain the virus. So, the best way to avoid the disease is to keep the virus out of the body.

Here are ways to prevent the presence of COVID-19 in your body.

- Avoid contact with people who have been infected with the virus. Wear gloves when you touch anything that could be contaminated by an infected person, such as a door handle or a phone.
- Infected patients need to have their rooms

regularly disinfected and washed down by a professional company. They shouldn't touch other people or their belongings without wearing a mask and gloves or clean up vomit without wearing goggles and rubber gloves.

- Avoid eating food that has been forgotten and leftovers in fridges – they might have been contaminated by viruses.
- When you know that you have come into close contact with someone who is infected (they sneezed or coughed on you, or came into contact with their vomit) – take a shower immediately. If you develop respiratory problems, fever and severe coughing do not hesitate to see a doctor as soon as possible.
- Patients must immediately disinfect their clothing, bed sheets, towels and wash with plenty of soap after they leave the hospital. Place all contaminated clothes or towels in sealed foil bags before throwing them away.
- If you have to visit a friend or relative in the hospital, take along your own personal protective equipment: clean, well-fitting disposable overalls, rubber gloves, and a face shield. Patients should also wear protective clothing.
- Try to avoid contact with person who are sick

or have been exposed to infected patients. People who have been exposed to being sneezed or coughed on the need to wash their hands immediately with soap and water after they leave the hospital. Wash yourself off thoroughly with water after you leave the hospital. If someone has been exposed to vomiting or diarrhea, then they will also need to wash their face and hands using soap and water after leaving the hospital.

- If there is any doubt about whether you have come into contact with someone who has COVID-19, then it is good to wear a face mask. If you must take your face mask off, then don't touch anything that has been in contact with the virus. Always try to cover your mouth when you cough or sneeze because viruses can be transmitted by breathing them in.
- Remember, if you have come into contact with the virus, wash your hands frequently.
- If you are pregnant, tell your doctor immediately. They will give you the best advice on how to prevent the virus from affecting your unborn baby. Make sure your partner knows that you are pregnant and that they should avoid close contact with people who are sick.
- If you have pets, wash your hands immediately

after touching your pets and don't touch or kiss your pets when you have a fever. Wash them with plenty of soap and warm water if they cough or sneeze.

- It's best to avoid shaking hands with anyone but if you need to shake someone's hand, make sure they wash their hands first. Also, make sure that their hands are dry. If someone has come into contact with an infected person, wash their hands immediately after shaking theirs.
- Do not kiss anyone or share things that could have been contaminated by a person who has COVID-19. It's also a great idea to avoid going to the beach or swimming pool as you can get infected with the virus from swimming in contaminated water.
- If you work in a hospital, rest area, clinic, or other medical facilities then it's important that you wear all of your personal protective equipment. This applies to those who work for pharmacies, banks, and other financial institutions too. Don't touch money if it was in contact with someone who has COVID-19.
- If you suspect that someone has COVID-19, or if you come into contact with the virus, it is good to isolate the infected person in an airtight room away from people. When you

isolate someone, cover their head with a face mask and wash them with soap and water after they leave.

HOW TO AVOID THE RISK OF SERIOUS SIDE EFFECTS FROM BEING EXPOSED TO THE VIRUS?

If you suspect that you have been exposed to the virus, there are several ways to avoid serious side effects.

One way is to get a vaccination. The vaccine does not provide immunity from the virus, but it can help prevent some of the serious side effects. The vaccination can help you avoid serious complications if you are exposed to the infection. The vaccine is recommended for anyone who is at risk of being exposed to the virus, including health care workers.

Try to reduce the number of viruses in your body. There are many different medications that can help prevent viruses from multiplying and spreading. The most common medication is interferon. Interferon is a protein that attacks the virus, prevents it from multiplying, and can prevent or reduce the severity of serious side effects. The medications, called antivirals, can also help stop the virus before it can spread to other parts of your body. There are so many different types of antiviral medicines available. Make sure that you take all of your medicine exactly as prescribed by your healthcare provider.

Improve your immune system so that it can better fight off the virus before it can cause serious damage. One of the most necessary things you can do is to eat a healthy diet. A healthy diet will provide your body with the vitamins and nutrients it needs to strengthen your immune system.

Another way of reducing the risk of serious side effects is to slow down the replication of the virus in your body by using antioxidants. Antioxidants slow down the replication of the virus because they interfere with the virus's ability to absorb iron. If the virus cannot efficiently absorb enough iron, it will not be able to reproduce and spread throughout your body. There are many natural substances that could be used as antioxidants; some of them include vitamin C, vitamin E, and glutathione. You can get these substances from foods such as broccoli and oranges, or you can get supplements like Lipovox.

Take anti-viral medications as prescribed by your doctor. These medications prevent and treat the infection and should be taken as soon as possible after you recover from potential exposure to the virus. There is no reason to delay taking anti-viral medications because of any thought that it may help to treat the infection or prevent future infections. If you take the medication and develop symptoms of an infection, seek medical attention immediately.

As always, drink enough fluids and stay hydrated. This prevents dehydration which may put you at risk for other diseases in addition to COVID-19. It is very necessary to stay hydrated and drinking plenty of fluids helps to keep your body temperature at a normal level and will prevent the onset of fevers.

6

HOW VACCINES WORKS

It's easy to imagine that vaccines are an effective form of medicine, but the science behind how they work is more complicated. Vaccines are made of living organisms that have been weakened or killed, which decreases the chance that you will catch the disease.

Vaccines contain active ingredients that can challenge your immune system in a controlled way and teach your body to fight off these foreign invaders.

Vaccines can be made from weakened live or killed organisms, just like the ones that cause disease. Live vaccines use weakened versions of the actual virus or bacteria that can cause infection. For example, if you get vaccinated against rubella (also called German measles), you are actually getting a small dose of the rubella virus. This does not make you sick, but it can make your immune system react in a way that produces antibodies to fight off the virus.

Killed or inactivated vaccines use only the parts of the organism that trigger an immune response, either by introducing a dead version of the virus or bacteria to your body, or by exposing you to a weakened form of it. If you're exposed to small amounts of killed virus over time, your body will respond by producing antibodies that fight that virus. This is what causes immunity against infection.

All vaccines contain an ingredient that causes your body to react in certain ways. This is called an "antigen." Antigens are either parts of the virus, bacteria, or bacterial toxins (poisons) that can cause illness. Some antigens are only recognized by your immune system if they are part of a microbe (like the measles virus or polio virus). Others can be recognized by your immune system on their own (like the tetanus toxin).

Vaccines contain antigens that:

> **Clump together:** When your body recognizes these antigens as foreign and attempts to fight them, the clumps (a.k.a. "immunogenic agents") form a substance called an antibody. Your immune system reacts to these substances as if

they were real germs, and produces antibodies to fight them off.

Make your body attack cancer cells: Antibodies prevent cancerous cells from growing and dividing. This is why vaccines often contain antigens that can produce antibodies that stop the growth and divide of cells that cause cancer.

Prevent the spread of disease: When an infection is present in or on your body, your immune system acknowledges it as a foreign invader and responds by producing antibodies to fight off infection. In this way, you develop fighting antibodies against the microbe or toxin in question, which gives you natural immunity against disease.

The number of doses that you need to get in order to become immune varies from vaccine to vaccine. For example, 3 doses of the hepatitis B vaccine are recommended for immunity against hepatitis B, while 8 doses of diphtheria, tetanus, and pertussis (DTaP) are recommended for diphtheria, tetanus, and pertussis. These numbers may seem high because booster shots (shots that you get after the initial vaccination) are needed to maintain active immunity against disease.

A few vaccines require fewer doses for immunity, which is why you only need the Tdap vaccine once after you turn 11 years old. However, immunity declines over time, which is why booster shots are recommended for certain diseases.

How long vaccines protect you from disease depends on the disease in question. Some vaccines last a lifetime, while others are only temporary. Many of them are recommended for children on a schedule to ensure they are up to date with their vaccinations.

Most vaccines are safe, but there are some concerns. For example, the human papilloma virus (HPV) vaccine has been associated with cases of severe pain, headache, and fatigue. This is why it's recommended only for girls and young women. Research is still being made to find out how long these symptoms can last or if they will go away on their own.

Some people report that they feel like they're getting sick after getting the flu shot. While this is very rare, it's important to know that there are other ways to prevent the flu, including getting vaccinated against it.

Vaccines also contain compound ingredients like:

> ***Antibodies:*** These proteins make your body and immune system fight and prevent infection and disease. People who get a vaccine containing an antigen with antibodies build up antibodies

against the microbe-producing antigen in the first 1-2 months after getting immunized.

Cell-mediated immunity: This is your natural, innate immune system. It works in conjunction with your antibodies to fight infections by producing immunoglobulin A (IgA), which coats your respiratory tract, digestive tract, etc., to prevent foreign objects from entering the body.

Toxoids: These are compounds that help you get rid of toxins, bacteria, fungi, and viruses. They contain antigens that are not cancer-causing agents but are strong "toxic" molecules. Once you receive a vaccine, your body recognizes these as "foreign" and it quickly produces antibodies to fight the toxins.

Why Vaccines Are Important

Vaccines can protect you from serious viruses, like measles and whooping cough. They can also prevent lifelong diseases like diphtheria (a debilitating disease that robs you of your voice and can even cause breathing problems) and tetanus (which can cause paralysis).

Vaccines are also important because they reduce the risk of transmission of disease to others. They can even lower the risk of certain types of cancer. For example, the HPV vaccine has been proven to prevent certain types of cancer (like cervical and vaginal cancer), and also genital warts.

What You Should Know Before Getting a Vaccine?

Vaccines are effective and safe, but there are some things you should consider before getting one. A few vaccines may be recommended for adults. Some vaccines require only a single shot; others require multiple doses or booster shots to maintain immunity and guard against disease.

After your first vaccination, you may get a fever, muscle aches, or mild swelling. This is normal, but it usually disappears within 2-3 days.

Your immune system will create antibodies against the vaccine's antigen for about 1-2 months after you get immunized. This happens because your immune system creates these antibodies in response to the vaccine itself. This is why you may feel sick for a few days after getting immunized. This is called an adverse reaction, and it occurs in 1-2% of people.

In rare cases, vaccines can cause serious reactions. These reactions commonly happen within a few hours or a few days after getting immunized. However, the reactions usually get better within 2-6 weeks after getting immunized.

Vaccines can also lead to mild side effects like:

Allergic reactions: These are the only vaccines that you should not get if you have some serious allergic reactions to any of the ingredients in them, such as latex (found in some rubber gloves and syringes), antibiotics, and thimerosal (a mercury-based preservative). When you think that you may be allergic to a vaccine, tell your doctor ahead of time.

Some people may notice that they get sick after receiving a vaccine. This is called an adverse reaction. It's important to know that reactions usually occur within a few hours or a few days after getting immunized. The most common reactions are:

If you have a severe reaction to the vaccine, get medical help right away. Parents should monitor their children closely for any problems after receiving a vaccine.

Other side effects may include:

Trouble breathing or shortness of breath: This is called an allergic reaction. It happens in about 1% of people, and it usually happens within 30 minutes to 6 hours after getting immunized. It can even happen after receiving only one dose. People who are allergic to the substances in the vaccine should not get it.

Tiredness: This usually goes away within 72

hours after getting immunized. Getting enough sleep and drinking lots of water can help you feel better when you're tired.
Sore arm: This is where the shot was given. It lasts for about 3 days, and it's normal to have redness, pain, or swelling at this spot.
Fever (more than 100°F): This is called an adverse reaction. It can happen after a vaccine, after a vaccination booster, or even a month afterwards. Getting plenty of rest and drinking lots of fluids may help you feel better when you have a fever.

When you have a serious allergic reaction to the vaccine, get medical help right away. Parents should monitor their children closely for any problems after receiving a vaccine.

Before getting vaccinated, some people may have some concerns about vaccines. These are the most common reasons why people don't get vaccinated:

Misconception #1: Vaccines are not safe.

Truth: Getting immunized is safer than getting the actual disease. Side effects from vaccines are usually mild and go away on their own. The most common adverse reactions from vaccines are usually fevers or sore arms from the shot.

Misconception #2: Vaccines cause autism.

Truth: Vaccines do not cause autism. Studies have shown this, but you may see people making statements about a vaccine-autism link on social media or other websites – even though no reputable scientific research has ever shown a link between vaccines and autism. Most studies have found that there is no link between vaccines and autism. The vaccine-autism claim was based on a study published in 1998 in the journal Lancet. On February 2, 2010, the medical journal Pediatrics published a study that showed that study's author had fudged his data. In March 2010, Lancet issued an official retraction of the article. In addition, a 2015 analysis of huge databases from several countries also found no link between vaccines and autism.

Misconception #3: Autism spectrum disorders (ASDs) are not caused by vaccines.

Truth: Research has shown that a child's risk of having an ASD is more than 7 times higher when they have a parent with an ASD, compared to a child without a parent with autism. In other words, the risk is biggest for kids born to moms with an ASD compared to kids without moms with autism. So, it's possible that there is a genetic loading factor from having a parent who has an ASD. Certain genetic disorders have been linked to ASDs, such as Fragile X syndrome and tuberous sclerosis. In a nutshell, a child with a parent with an ASD is more likely to develop an ASD than a child with no affected family members.

Misconception #4: I've already had the measles/mumps/whooping cough/rubella (MMR), so I don't need to get vaccinated.

Truth: Most people receive all of their recommended vaccinations by the time they are 12 years old, but this is not true for everyone. Vaccinating your children can help protect them from severe diseases like measles or whooping cough.

Misconception #5: My doctor said vaccines are dangerous and I should be skeptical about anything she tells me.

Truth: Your doctor is trained to give medical advice, so she or he can't guarantee that any one way of treating you will be the best way. However, your doctor's advice to you is based on the best available evidence and the doctor's experience with your specific condition. When it comes to vaccines, doctors take an oath to put their patients first and do what is in their best interest.

People should always talk to a doctor regarding any concerns they may have about vaccines.

HOW VACCINES PROTECTS US FROM COVID-19

The best way to protect oneself from COVID-19 is to take Covid-19 vaccines. Anti-covid vaccinations are like any other vaccination: they train your immune system and create antibodies to fight off certain viruses and bacteria. By making your immune system train to recognize and fight off this particular form of the covid virus, your body will never get its hands on it.

Anti-covid are made using special, biological processes that can identify specific proteins or cells that are attacking us. The anti-covid then act like antibodies; they respond to these foreign items (i.e., viruses), neutralizing them before they can make us sick.

COVID-19 vaccine are completely safe, provided that they are administered correctly. You should not be concerned about getting sick from a COVID-19 vaccination.

COVID-19 vaccines work by preventing the virus from reactivating in different parts of your body, which would cause you to get sick again. It also helps to make sure that you don't infect other people and spread the virus around.

Once a virus infects a cell, it changes the DNA in the cell, but some of the DNA remains. The DNA that does stay in place is CDR or core promoter region of a virus.

The COVID-19 vaccine prevents this from happening by producing antibodies against this region of DNA. As well as producing antibodies to prevent infection, your body releases proteins called cytokines. These are proteins that act like messengers to tell other cells in your body to make more lymphocytes (cells that make antibodies). A high number of lymphocytes in your body means that you can fight off infection.

It typically takes a few weeks after vaccination for the body to produce T-lymphocytes and B-lymphocytes. These are the specialized cells in the immune system. The B-lymphocytes produce antibodies that fight against specific bacteria, viruses or other microorganisms. While the T-lymphocytes are responsible for killing the pathogens directly.

The immune system has to take time to 'remember' the face of the virus so it can clear it away when it appears in your body. That's why it takes time to get protected by a COVID-19 vaccine. But once you do get protected, your body already has an army of cells to take care of the virus. The army will keep attacking the virus for as long as it can. When the virus is completely destroyed, your immune system has the ability to remember the face of that virus and will attack it much quicker next time.

The antibodies that produced by the COVID-19 vaccine are raised against this region but are not able to attack it directly. Your immune system is then alerted to produce more lymphocytes that kill the virus in its cells. A healthy response to the vaccine is observed in the people who received it (98% of people who received it had a good response, according to some studies).

COVID-19 vaccine Side Effects

COVID-19 vaccines are very safe. Side effects are mild, including temporary pain at the injection site (about 12% of people experience this), mild fever (less than 2%) and swollen glands (less than 8%).

Allergic reactions to vaccines are rare, and they can happen in anyone, even in people who have had the vaccine before. Most side effects from the COVID-19 vaccine occur in people who have not been vaccinated before.

These side effects are commonly only temporary and may go away by themselves in a few days or can be managed with rest or over-the-counter medications.

COVID-19 vaccine is safe. Because the anti-COVID-19 virus can affect you in different ways, it's important to make sure that the vaccine really works and is safe before you get it.

Before you receive anti-COVID-19 vaccination, your healthcare provider will give you a series of tests. These tests will include looking at your immune system and blood work to make sure that this vaccine is right for you.

When you have had a serious allergic reaction to any vaccine in the past, then you should not get this vaccine. Your healthcare provider shall determine if this is appropriate for you. Though, you should know that people who have had serious reactions to the anti-COVID-19 virus are not common.

7

TYPES OF VACCINES

So, you want to be a responsible person and get vaccinated, but you're wondering which ones? The great news is that there are different types of vaccines to choose from, depending on your needs. The four types are:

Inactivated Virus Vaccines

This is the classic, simple and easy to use vaccine. The inactivated virus vaccines contain virus which has been killed (usually in various ways such as heat or chemicals) rendering it inert and without the ability to cause disease. Post-Vaccination Immunity

This is when you get vaccinated and your body builds up immunity for at least a few weeks after the injection. This immunity lasts up to 21 days in most cases, but it can last somewhat longer in some cases and in some areas, and much shorter elsewhere. The time it lasts can vary due to many factors. This type of immunity is relatively short-lived but makes the need for boosters rare, usually only needing one to two injections during your life span.

Live Attenuated Vaccines (LAV)

This virus is live but has been weakened so that it cannot cause disease. This vaccine is approved for people with weakened immune systems because this type of vaccine causes the body to build up actual immunity rather than relying on post-vaccination protection like inactivated vaccines do. Live vaccines are highly effective and highly recommended for people with weakened immune systems. However, since they are live viruses, they can be dangerous to the very young, the very old or those with weakened immune systems. For this reason, most LAV cannot be used on pregnant women. This type of vaccine is also not recommended for most women of child-bearing age due to the risk of passing it along to their babies during birth. In some cases, it can be given during pregnancy, but only if absolutely necessary and with strict precautions.

Put simply: the more at risk you are for disease, the more likely it is that you should be given a live attenuated (LAV) vaccine.

Benefits of LAV

This type of vaccine is very effective, in some cases 90 percent or more, in stopping the spread of disease. This type of vaccine is also used in conjunction with other vaccines when it's needed. It's also less painful than many other vaccines, which can be beneficial to small babies or elderly people that are tender-headed.

Fewer side effects than some other vaccines that contain live viruses get vaccinated even without actually having the disease you are protecting yourself from. Note that this does not mean that you will get the disease from this type of vaccine, but it can cause a mild reaction in some people. It's also not recommended to vaccinate a child with a live vaccine unless it is absolutely necessary. This is because children are more vulnerable to diseases and complications from them, and they should wait until their immune systems are stronger before getting vaccinations.

Protein-Based Vaccines

This type of vaccine is made either with actual bacteria, or it is made by injecting or injecting the material into dead bacteria. This type of vaccine is used to produce antibodies that fight infection caused by the actual bacteria itself. Antibodies are proteins that our immune system creates to identify and build up protection against certain diseases.

While these vaccines do not contain actual live viruses, they are very effective at stopping the spread of infection caused by their target bacterium, though not as high as LAV might be. This type of vaccine is also less effective than LAV in protecting people with weakened immune systems, children under the age of 4, and those who are pregnant or breastfeeding.

Due to their effectiveness, most people choose this type of vaccine over LAV.

Benefits of protein-based vaccines

This type of vaccine is very effective at treating infections caused by bacteria (such as staph infections like Staphylococcus aureus). It's also very effective at preventing infection caused by bacteria (such as strep throat). This type of vaccine helps protect people both with strong and weakened immune systems because it does not cause the complications that LAV does.

This type of vaccination causes fewer side effects than some other vaccines.

Protein-based vaccines are recommended for people with weakened immune systems, children under the age of 4, and pregnant women or breastfeeding mothers.

Viral Vector Vaccines

Viral Vector COVID-19 vaccines are being clinically tested by the vaccine companies AstraZeneca and Merck. These vaccines are based on the technology of viral vectorization. They are designed with recombinant DNA to insert genes into certain viruses. Viral vector vaccines are also being researched for their potential to treat cancer, HIV infection, hepatitis B, chickenpox, small pox and the herpes virus.

This type of vaccine carries healthy genes to areas of the body where they can stimulate the immune system with healthy proteins and trigger an immune response against disease-causing pathogens or cancers instead.

They are also being researched to treat cancer, HIV infection, hepatitis B, chickenpox, small pox and the herpes virus.

Although this type of vaccine does not contain the actual viruses themselves, they can be extremely effective at fighting disease-causing pathogens.

Immunocompromised patients are very susceptible to viral vector vaccines since these types of vaccinations are designed to help the immune system fight diseases without harming healthy cells.

The viral vector vaccines contain a 'vector' that helps the immune system learn how to fight diseases.

Benefits of vaccine vectorization

Viral vector vaccines can stimulate the immune system to fight disease causing pathogens and cancers. These types of vaccines have been proven to be more effective than traditional vaccines, which have been shown to not only contain dead viruses from the diseases they are designed to battle, but also can sometimes cause temporary problems in people's bodies by building up too much immunity as well as causing temporary side effects.

Because viral vector vaccines do not contain the actual viruses, they can be safe and effective for immunocompromised individuals.

Viral vector vaccines are also more effective in some cases than the live attenuated (LAV) type of vaccine.

Genetic Vaccines: mRNA and DNA

These vaccines are based on an mRNA (messenger RNA) or DNA (deoxyribonucleic acid) that carries genes into the body. These sorts of vaccines fight infection by producing antibodies that fight infection caused by specific pathogens. To create mRNA or DNA vaccines, the gene is taken from a contaminated person and used to make its own version of the pathogen, which is then injected into a person. The natural immune system will recognize this pathogen as being foreign and attack it, resulting in an immune response against it.

This is the newest type of vaccine. This is also one of the safest as it is very unlikely to cause side effects. Because it uses a person's own genetic material, this vaccine can be targeted at a specific group, which decreases the chance that a person will have an allergic reaction or other complications from vaccination. Genetic vaccines are also more effective at stimulating a strong immune response against certain diseases and illnesses.

There are a variety of vaccines in clinical trials. Vaccines in clinical trials may be experimental vaccines or new types of existing vaccines. Research studies in humans to determine how safe a vaccine is and whether it can help prevent a disease. Clinical trials are run in phases, usually in three phases. Phase I, Phase II, and Phase III can take from several months to many years to complete. Clinical trials usually involve healthy subjects. These people volunteer to participate in the clinical trials and receive an injection, which is usually a vaccine or other preparation that has not been proven effective for preventing disease.

Clinical trials are sometimes used to test safety and effectiveness before a vaccine is approved for widespread use.

There are a number of reasons why a vaccine study might need volunteers. Examples include:

> Either way, no vaccine is 100% effective. Even with a complete vaccination schedule, most people will not be protected from disease forever. However, vaccines have been very effective in stopping the spread of disease and have saved millions lives worldwide. Thanks to vaccines, smallpox has been wiped from the earth and cases of polio have been reduced by 99%. Whooping cough is also at a historic low in the United States with only 9 cases in 2011. Vaccines play a vital role in protecting and preserving global health. It is important to remember that it takes time for vaccines to produce results; they take 2–5 years to prevent disease, and between 14 and 20 years to eradi-

> cate an infection from the human population, based on the World Health Organization (WHO). Vaccines prevent disease before symptoms appear. If infected people are not vaccinated, they will spread the virus and infect others, which could lead to some serious complications like pneumonia or meningitis.

In the United States, the Food and Drug Administration (FDA) is responsible for monitoring vaccine safety. They increase vaccine safety by monitoring the development of new vaccines to ensure that they are safe and effective before being used in a clinical trial or on a large scale. They also review information from clinical trials and post marketing surveillance, a type of research that looks at how well a vaccine works after it has been released for public use. The FDA approves vaccines after they have gone through phase I, which involves safety testing to see if the vaccine causes any adverse side effects. Phase II involves preliminary safety and efficacy testing, and phase III involves larger scale studies in large groups of people to see if the vaccine works better than it did in initial trials. People who are really interested in enrolling in clinical trials must contact their local health office for more information.

Vaccines can be either injected or taken by mouth (via tablets). Many vaccines are given to children orally, but adults also receive several vaccines through an injection. The majority of vaccines available in the US are given as an injection, but there are also a number of vaccines that can be taken by mouth.

Most vaccine doses are given in a 2-dose regimen. Two months after the first injection, children receive a booster shot, which contains all three recommended childhood vaccines at one time. For adults, the most common childhood vaccines are measles-mumps-rubella (MMR) and chickenpox. Adults receive a booster shot that includes MMR, varicella (chickenpox), tetanus, diphtheria, and pertussis (whooping cough). There are also some adults who choose to get vaccines separately. A small number of vaccines are given as an injection only. These include the influenza vaccine, pneumococcal conjugate vaccine (PCV) for children older than 2 months, and human papilloma virus (HPV).

Most adults 65 years or older also receive the same series of vaccines as children. Vaccines protect you from certain harmful illnesses. They do not guarantee that you will not get sick, but they can help prevent certain problems.

TYPES OF VACCINES FOR COVID-19

There are three major approaches to designing a vaccine.

1. One approach is to produce a vaccine with the virus or bacteria that causes the disease.
2. A second approach is to synthesize part of the virus or bacteria and use it as a vaccine.
3. The third approach uses components of the body's immune system called antibodies, which protect against infections, as a vaccine—or "immunity.

Researchers use different approaches to create vaccines, and some vaccines work better than others. This is especially true in the case of live viruses and bacteria that are used as vaccines. Your immune system should be able to acknowledge the foreign body that has been injected into the body in order for it to be effective. Otherwise, you could have an immune response that would react against the vaccine itself.

These are the common types of Vaccines:

There are two main kinds of vaccine that could be used to fight off any potential covid from the COVID-19 virus.

The first type of anti-covid is a live, attenuated vaccine. This means that the vaccine has been changed from its natural, harmful state to a weaker form of itself. This weaker form will still teach your immune system to recognize and fight off harmful viruses and bacteria, but it will not make you sick in the process.

This type of anti-covid contains a "weakened virus." This weakened virus is able to reach your immune system, which will then start producing anti-bodies. The vaccine itself does not cause any harm because it has been weakened so that it is incapable of replicating or even spreading further.

The second type of anti-covid is a killed, inactivated vaccine. This type of anti-covid works by using very small doses of harmful viruses or bacteria to stimulate the immune system.

This is done by using minute amounts of these germs, called antigens. The body then makes antibodies in response to these antigens.

However, there are not enough antigens to cause disease. This means that the vaccines are harmless since they only contain minute amounts of toxins.

You will need to take anti-covid vaccinations if you want to protect yourself from COVID-19. By taking these vaccines, your immune system will be trained to recognize the antigens found in the COVID-19 virus, making it impossible for your body to get sick.

WHAT COVID-19 VACCINES HAVE BEEN AUTHORIZED?

The data should show that the vaccines are safe and effective before the FDA can give emergency use authorization. Vaccines with FDA emergency use authorization include:

Pfizer-BioNTech COVID-19 vaccine

The Pfizer-BioNTech COVID-19 vaccine is 95% effective in preventing the COVID-19 virus with symptoms. In addition, it is also able to suppress the development of symptoms caused by COVID-19 infection within the body. This effect is especially important to prevent secondary infections. It requires two injections given 21 days apart. The second dose might be given up to six weeks after the first dose.

Moderna COVID-19 vaccine.

The Moderna COVID-19 vaccine is 94% effective in preventing the COVID-19 virus with symptoms. This vaccine was also highly effective in clinical trials at preventing COVID-19. It requires three injections, which must be given 28 days apart. The Moderna vaccine is recommended for persons aged 18 and over.

Janssen/Johnson & Johnson COVID-19 vaccine

The Janssen/Johnson & Johnson COVID-19 vaccine is 66% effective in preventing the COVID-19 virus. It has been licensed for use to prevent COVID-19 infection in adults aged 18 and over. It requires one injection.

WHAT COVID-19 VACCINE HAS BEEN APPROVED FOR KIDS?

US Food and Drug Administration (FDA) has granted emergency use authorization to the Pfizer-BioNTech COVID-19 vaccination for youth aged 12 to 15. This vaccine, now known as Comirnaty, has also been licensed by the FDA to prevent COVID-19 in people aged 16 and up.

The COVID-19 vaccine from Pfizer and BioNTech requires two shots spaced 21 days apart. If it is necessary, the second dose may be given up to six weeks following the first.

Pfizer-BioNTech COVID-19 vaccine has been established to be 100 percent effective in preventing COVID-19 in children aged 12 to 15. In people aged 16 and up, the vaccine is 91 percent effective in avoiding serious COVID-19 sickness. According to a preliminary study, the vaccination is 96 percent effective in preventing serious COVID-19 disease caused by the delta form, which is currently the most frequent COVID-19 variant in the United States.

8

EMPOWERING EVERYONE WITH KNOWLEDGE OF THEIR IMMUNITY

The immune system is considered as the most complex system in our body. It protects us from infection, virus, and other diseases. Our body's natural defenses are very effective in fighting bacteria, viruses, and fungi. But these threats don't always respect the boundaries of our body's structures, so it is important to understand how our immune system works for us to understand what we should do when it is not working well.

A HISTORY OF THE HUMAN IMMUNE SYSTEM

The human immune system has an interesting history. It can be traced back to more than 100 years ago, when the first type of immune system was discovered. The discovery helped scientists understand how the body protected itself against diseases, and it also allowed them to come up with cures for certain ailments.

The immune system is what helps keep people healthy. Without an immune system, people would get sick all of the time and they could die within a few days of getting sick. The human body has gone through many different changes over its life, but the immune system has remained unchanged. Antibodies are still used by the immune system to fight off disease, and they have always been part of the body's defense against infection.

The first discovery of an immune system happened in 1884, when a scientist stumbled upon white blood cells that fought infection. While it was interesting to find these cells in the body, nobody knew exactly how they worked or why they existed. When scientists began to research the immune system, they made a breakthrough. They figured out that white blood cells helped to fight off disease and infections. While this was an important discovery, it didn't come until much later when scientists made another discovery.

In 1930, researchers discovered antibodies and what they did. They discovered that antibodies attacked pathogens and stopped them from harming the body. From there, science began to learn more about how antibodies attacked harmful organisms. As technology improved, science discovered new methods for fighting disease, including vaccines and antibiotics.

In 1935, scientists discovered how the human immune system worked. It was a slow process, as scientists had to learn about the body and its individual parts. Other research has helped scientists learn a lot about how the body fights off disease and protects against infection. The immune system is a complicated system that scientists have only just begun to understand completely.

Immune systems have been categorized by many different factors, including age, race and gender. While a lot of research has been done, scientists still have a lot to learn about the human body and how it functions. People have learned a lot about the immune system because it's so important for keeping people healthy. It's important for people to take care of their bodies, as they rely on the immune system to stay well. People can protect themselves against illnesses by washing their hands and being careful with germs.

THE IMMUNE SYSTEM'S ROLE IN PREVENTING COVID-19

Our human immune system is made up of a variety of cells and organs. It works to keep the body healthy, by preventing disease. While it may seem confusing, the immune system is actually quite simple. The main job of the immune system is to protect people against disease, but it also helps them recover from an illness faster. The human cell contains receptors that are used to defend against viruses and bacteria that can cause harm to the body. The immune system also uses antibodies to protect against foreign invaders, and also helps the body to fight off certain diseases. One way that it makes this is through starting a response as soon as the invader is identified. The immune system does not have any choice but to react quickly, or else it could be too late to protect against disease.

When the immune system is healthy, it fights off diseases and infection much more efficiently. While there are certain diseases that are harmless or need no treatment at all, others can cause severe damage if left untreated. When people have a weak immune system, they can get sick easily and succumb to dangerous diseases if they don't get treatment.

People should know the parts of the immune system and how they work together in order to keep themselves healthy. It's important to know exactly how the body works, including all of its organs and cells, in order to understand all of its systems. The body's immune system can be broken down into different sections that work together to protect against different types of disease. For example, the lymph nodes are parts of the immune system that help protect against diseases by trapping harmful substances. The spleen works with the lymph nodes to filter out substances that can hurt the body. Another part of the immune system is the skin, which helps keep people safe from outside invaders by defending against germs and bacteria on a regular basis. The skin also helps get rid of any impurities that are harmful to the body.

The immune system is an important part of keeping people healthy. If a person understands how it works, they'll be able to take advantage of all the ways that it keeps them safe from dangerous diseases. It's very important for people to practice good hygiene and take care of their bodies, as even a tiny mistake could cause serious problems.

WHAT IS THE IMMUNE SYSTEM?

The immune system is a complex network of organs and cells that together protect us from invading microbes and help us fight back when we accidentally bump into them.

How does it work?

The parts of our immune system include: white blood cells, the lymphatic system, and the central nervous system. Once we are already exposed to a pathogen (the enemy), our body activates the following systems:

1. The skin is the first line of defense against germs.
2. The white blood cells (WBCs) in our circulation detect the presence of germs and start to fight them by releasing antimicrobial proteins that destroy the invading microbe.
3. Lymphatic system is made up of lymph nodes, lymph ducts, and lymph vessels which contain white blood cells (lymphocytes) that help fight against germs in another location (different part of the body).
4. The central nervous system (the brain and the spinal cord) coordinates and directs all of these defense resources.

How is it organized?

Immune system is made up of various types of cells and tissues. There are three main divisions:

1. The innate immune system: this part of our body's defenses is always ready to fight

invaders, because it does not need to be "trained" to recognize harmful invaders.

2. The adaptive immune system: this part of our body's defenses is trained to recognize and fight invaders, because the training precedes the actual encounter with an invader.
3. The somatic (body) immune system: it is present only during childhood, adolescence, and early adulthood. This is usually made up of white blood cells that fight pathogens in our body by releasing antimicrobial proteins that destroy the invading microbe.

The first line of defense: skin

The skin is the first line of defense against germs. If germs are ingested, these defenses are reinforced through the intestinal tract. The skin maintains a strong barrier against attackers, including dangerous microorganisms. The first encounter with dangerous germs is usually the strongest one. This explains why we get sick after traveling to a different country or population group where some diseases which were previously unknown to us are widespread.

The skin is the first line of defense against germs because it contains:

1. Epidermis: a protective barrier against invading microorganisms. It is made up of dead cells that do not contain any bacterium, virus or fungus.
2. Dermis: a vascular network that transports food and oxygen to the epidermis cells and transports waste away from them.
3. Sebaceous glands: these glands make a fatty substance called sebum which keeps our skin lubricated and waterproofed. This also prevents water loss through the skin. This oily substance contains antibacterial compounds, including cholesterol and fatty acids. It is a major component of our natural skin-barrier and helps fight infections and pathogens, as well as sunburns.

Our second line of defense: white blood cells

White blood cells (WBCs) are very important communication agents in our body's defense system.

They cover all the body's surfaces, such as:

1. The mouth and nose
2. Nasal passages and sinuses
3. Ears and throat
4. Eyes and eyelids
5. Mouth and stomach

6. Blood vessels, lungs and intestines
7. Skin and other surfaces
8. The entire body surface (including the mucous membranes)

There are two different types of white blood cells: B-cells and T-cells. The B-cell produces antibodies that can destroy microorganisms that invade into our body through the first line of defense: the skin. The T-cell is made up of two different types: memory T-cells and effector T-cells. The memory T-cells help the body remember the microbe that was encountered in a previous fight, so that a quick response can be triggered when a pathogen attempts to enter our body again. The effector T-cells are responsible for destroying pathogens by releasing toxic substances, such as:

1. Interferons
2. Interleukins
3. The enzyme cytotoxic granule protein
4. The protein perforin
5. Other well-known molecules, such as hydrogen peroxide, TNF-alpha and nitric oxide

The lymphatic system: the second line of defense

The lymph nodes are small structures made up of white blood cells, which carry lymph (white blood cells and plasma) from the various tissues to the bloodstream where they can be transported all over the body. The lymph vessels are the only ones in our body that contain WBCs.

An important function of the lymphatic system is to produce lymphocytes, which are white blood cells that help fight against germs in other body regions (different parts). The central nervous system is able to remember dangerous microbes, so when they enter our body again, the memory T-cells will be activated to quickly destroy them.

Why our immunity is important?

Our immunity is a very important part of our body's defense system against pathogenic organisms so that we can stay healthy and avoid many diseases. Some infections have been curbed by immunization against them. This is why vaccines are so important.

Approximately, there are between 400 and 500 different kinds of germs (and harmful viruses) which can cause diseases such as: an infection, a disease, a cancer, or an auto-immune disorder. Our immunity can fight hundreds of different types of microbes and even more if we include its memory T-cells.

The immune system is very delicate, if our immunity is not strong enough, it cannot destroy all the microorganisms that are present in the environment. However, our immune system also needs to do its job properly in order to protect us. Therefore, we must make sure our immunity is active and present in order to fight off infections.

The good way to boost the body's immunity is by taking your vitamins. Every day we ingest several nutrients that can support or encourage our immune system. Some of these include: vitamins A, B and C and minerals such as zinc, selenium and magnesium. We also ingest many different substances that can help our immune system: certain fatty acids (such as omega-3), amino acids (such as tryptophan), carbohydrates (such as lactose) and others.

When the body is exposed to microorganisms such as viruses or bacteria, they can then trigger certain molecules to be released into our blood.

Vaccines are also able to stimulate the immune system by stimulating the memory T-cells. This is because they contain substances that can stimulate specific cells within our immune system. For example, the body's immune system recognizes viruses as foreign objects that need to be destroyed. When a person receives a vaccination against a virus (such as polio), his or her immune system will thereafter remember this microbe and activate special antibodies in order to capture it and destroy it.

Vaccines can also stimulate our immune system by giving birth to new antibodies. These new antibodies are created in the blood after the person receives a vaccination, and they can then fight against other germs that enter our blood.

Another way vaccines stimulate our immune system is by stimulating the memory T-cells. This activation of our T-cells can help us develop an immunity to given infectious diseases, which will help fight them in the future should they run into us again.

If a vaccine is given to a person who has been only moderately exposed to a virus, the immune system will not be able to process it. This means that the immune system will not be able to create antibodies or memory T-cells against it. However, if a person has been seriously exposed to a virus, the body's immune system might already contain antibodies and memory T-cells that have been stimulated from previous infections. Thus, the immune system will be able to fight the virus effectively.

SARS-CoV-2 virus is the "invisible" microbe. It has been classified as a coronavirus, which is a group of viruses that cause respiratory and other infections in humans. Our immune system can recognize SARS-CoV-2 virus as a dangerous outside invader, but the virus tricks it by entering into our body through the mucous membranes of the eyes or mouth. The central nervous system can "remember" this pathogen, so when SARS-CoV-2 enters our body again, our memory T-cells are activated to immediately destroy it.

COVID-19 vaccine is a human anti-coronavirus vaccine. It protects us from the effects of SARS-CoV-2 virus. It helps our immune system recognize and destroy "the invisible enemy" before it gets a chance to attack.

The trial results showed that anti covid vaccines helped protect against SARS-CoV-2. This human anti-coronavirus vaccine is especially useful for people traveling to areas where SARS-CoV-2 is widespread. It might also be used to help prevent the spread of the virus.

If you want to avoid spreading the virus being vaccinated against SARS-CoV-2 virus, is the best way to do so. Vaccine has no any serious side effects and it has undergone a lot of rigorous trials and tests before it was licensed for use.

SARS-CoV-2 virus is a dangerous invisible enemy that we all have to be very careful about. If we get infected, not only will we suffer from the sickness virus causes, but we will also spread the disease to others. However, with this vaccine, we may be able to protect ourselves against the disease. This human anti-coronavirus vaccine will help protect our bodies' immunity so that we can stay healthy and avoid many diseases which can be caused by SARS-CoV-2 virus.

9

CORONAVIRUS AND PREGNANCY: WHAT YOU SHOULD KNOW

TIPS FOR PREGNANT WOMEN

If you are pregnant, then it's important to follow the doctor's instructions the best that you can. If you are not yet 6 weeks pregnant, then take your temperature once in a while. Always remember that it's better to be safe than sorry.

Infection from COVID-19 is particularly dangerous for pregnant women. The people who are pregnant or recently pregnant are more probably to be severely ill with COVID-19 compared with the people who are not pregnant. That is why it's so important for pregnant women to get vaccinated against the virus. It's also important that pregnant women take better care of themselves when they are sick. Make sure that you don't let your condition get worse.

Get to a doctor as soon as you can if you can't breathe or can't stop coughing. It's very crucial for pregnant women to get their condition checked by a professional, especially if you start feeling like something is going wrong with your body. The symptoms just might be from COVID-19.

The evidence about the safety and effectiveness of COVID-19 vaccination during pregnancy has been increasing. The number of pregnant women who are vaccinated against the virus is increasing.

When you are planning on getting pregnant, then it's also very important that you get yourself vaccinated.

Although the vaccine is very safe for pregnant women, you should still take it under your doctor's supervision.

Vaccines contain a little percentage of the virus' active ingredients. The amount is not harmful, but it still depends on a person's immune system to react properly to the vaccine. If your immune system does not respond properly, then you might have a vaccine reaction or have some side effects from the vaccine.

There is one more thing that pregnant women should take into consideration. Getting sick with COVID-19 will greatly affect their pregnancy. We still have limited information about whether COVID-19 in particular is connected with pregnancy loss, miscarriage or stillbirth but it is a possibility because high fevers in pregnancy, particularly in the first trimester, could raise the risk of birth defects. That is why we encourage our patients to protect themselves from any illness that causes fever, including the flu.

AVOIDING THE CORONAVIRUS DURING PREGNANCY

People who are infected with COVID-19 can also easily spread it to pregnant women who are around them. Pregnant women must not go out of their way to prevent themselves from getting sick with the Coronavirus by wearing face masks, because it's too dangerous for their own health and the baby growing inside of them.

Pregnant women are more susceptible to getting severely ill with COVID-19. It's not just because they are pregnant, but also because of the way their body reacts to illness during pregnancy.

When you compare your risks of getting infected with another respiratory virus like the Influenza virus (flu), then it's obvious that it's very much worth taking precautionary measures against COVID-19 because it has a large potential to harm you and your baby during pregnancy.

As a pregnant woman, you should take extra care of yourself and avoid any infections as much as possible. Vaccinating against the Coronavirus is a must because it can cause serious illnesses, including respiratory issues. Pregnant women should not worry too much about getting vaccinated because the vaccine is very safe to take to protect themselves from this virus, but still make sure that you keep a proper hygiene and do not allow anyone to cough or sneeze on you.

There is a lot of evidence showing the safety and effectiveness of COVID-19 vaccination during pregnancy, but still make sure that you get yourself vaccinated under the supervision of your doctor because no vaccine is 100% safe.

THE SAFETY AND EFFICACY OF COVID-19 VACCINATION IN PREGNANCY

There is a lot of evidence that shows the safety and effectiveness of COVID-19 vaccination during pregnancy, but you should still get yourself vaccinated under the supervision of your doctor.

Vaccinating against Coronavirus during pregnancy is very important and will greatly protect yourself and your unborn child from getting infected with the virus. Pregnant women should not worry too much about getting vaccinated because the vaccine is very safe to take to protect themselves from this virus.

Below is a brief summary of the increasing evidence:

1. COVID-19 vaccines do not cause COVID-19 infection, including in people who are pregnant or their babies.

2. Vaccination against COVID-19 in pregnant women has been studied in various ways. The vaccine has been very safe for them because no serious side effects have been reported to date.

3. Vaccination does not increase the risk of miscarriage or stillbirth in pregnant women, or cause fetal loss during the first trimester of pregnancy when there are many other causes for these complications.

4. Vaccination does not seem to increase the risk of birth defects, especially in pregnant women or their babies.

5. Early data on the safety of receiving an mRNA COVID-19 vaccine (Moderna or Pfizer-BioNTech) during pregnancy are reassuring.

Early data suggest that receiving an mRNA COVID-19 vaccine during pregnancy decreases the risk for infection. Recent studies from Israel compared the individuals who were pregnant and received an mRNA COVID-19 vaccine with the people who did not. Scientists also found that vaccination lowered the risk of infection from the virus that causes COVID-19.

6. No adverse pregnancy-related outcomes occurred in previous clinical trials that used the same vaccine platform as the J&J/Janssen COVID-19 vaccine. This is a summary of the safety and effectiveness of COVID-19 vaccination during pregnancy, but you should still get vaccinated under the supervision of your doctor.

PEOPLE WHO ARE BREASTFEEDING

Vaccination during pregnancy is especially important for women who are breastfeeding because they would be at higher risks to get sick with COVID-19 and transmit it to their baby.

There is a huge evidence that shows the safety and effectiveness of COVID-19 vaccination during pregnancy, but still make sure that you get vaccinated under the supervision of your doctor.

COVID-19 vaccines that are currently used in the United States did not include people who are breastfeeding. Previous reports have also shown that breast-feeding people who have received mRNA COVID-19 vaccines have antibodies in their breast milk, which can help protect their babies. More data are needed to know the level of protection these antibodies can provide to the baby.

10

WHAT ARE THE BENEFITS OF BEING VACCINATED AGAINST COVID-19?

COVID-19 is a type of virus that's a member of the family called Corona Virus and it is usually mild, but it can lead to complications in some cases, such as bronchitis or pneumonia.

The most usual reason for people to be vaccinated against COVID-19 is so they can avoid these complications, particularly for those who have asthma, chronic lung disease, allergies, or other health conditions that would make them more probably to experience complications from COVID-19. In people who suffer from asthma, a complication from COVID-19 can cause a narrowing of the airways and make it difficult to breathe. If a person's lungs already have been weakened because of an underlying illness, the virus can become a serious problem for them.

Another reason people are vaccinated against COVID-19 is so they can avoid getting sick during the cold season. During this time of year, people are in closer contact with each other than usual, so they're more likely to spread germs. When a person has an underlying health condition or weakened lungs, they could become sicker than usual during the winter. As a result, doctors sometimes recommend that their patients get vaccinated against COVID-19 during the cold season.

Another reason is that they can avoid catching it from their pet. People who have a cat or dog at home may be more likely to spread the virus. They could spread it either by touching a surface that a cat or dog was on and then touching their own face or by coming into close contact with a cat or dog's saliva, such as when they're kissing them. But cats and dogs can also get sick from catching the virus from people. In this case, the person would need to get vaccinated against COVID-19 to prevent them from passing it on to their pet.

In some places, people who work with animals, such as barnyard animals or farm animals, might be more probably to come into contact with the virus. Because of this, it's a good idea for them to get vaccinated against COVID-19. The symptoms of the virus are not usually very severe and most people who catch it from an animal recover completely within a few days. But if a person is working with animals and they do become infected, it could cause the person to be very sick and they may need to stay in the hospital.

Another reason people get vaccinated against COVID-19 is so they can avoid catching it from someone who's been exposed to it. Someone who's been exposed to the virus can be contagious even after they've recovered. To protect themselves from catching the virus, some people will recommend that their family members get vaccinated as well. In this case, it's a good idea for everyone in the household, including any children, to get vaccinated against COVID-19.

Individuals who live or work in places where there are a lot of people, like hospitals, nursing homes, and schools, are also at higher risk of catching the virus. Because of this, some people may want to talk to their doctor about getting vaccinated against COVID-19.

These vaccines also help keep you from being seriously ill even if you do get COVID-19.

If you have the virus but have been vaccinated against it, you are much less likely to develop complications from the virus. Also, if you've had the virus before and were vaccinated against it, you are much less likely to get it again.

Being vaccinated can help you avoid passing the virus to other people. This can be especially helpful if you have a weakened immune system because of a health condition, like asthma or chronic lung disease, or because you are taking medicines that make your immune system weaker. People with weakened immune systems are more probably to become seriously ill from the virus. Also, they're more likely to pass it along to others who might not have a strong enough immune system to fight it off.

11

ALTERNATIVE WAYS OF PREVENTING COVID-19 INFECTION

There are also a number of things people could do to prevent themselves from contracting COVID-19, with most of the prevention methods focusing on education and prevention.

The COVID-19 epidemic has been one of the most prominent global events to happen in recent years. Despite the eradication efforts made, it has now become a pandemic that is currently threatening all major regions of the world.

Fortunately, as researchers have managed to find a cure for the disease, they have also identified alternative ways of preventing infection from taking place.

Since the disease is most commonly contracted by breathing in unfiltered air containing COVID-19, it is important to make sure that people are using an effective dust filter in their environment. Some of the most common filters on the market today include HEPA filters, activated carbon filters, and electrostatic filters. However, as these filters are easily removable from most household appliances, it is important to ensure they are cleaned on a regular basis.

Although it is uncommon for animals to carry COVID-19, it is still important for people to make sure that their pets are also wearing a mask when they are outside. Most of the time, pets contract the disease by licking themselves, which can make it easier for them to transmit the virus.

One way to prevent infection with COVID-19 is by using protective clothing, equipment, and facilities. This includes using equipment that is designed to contain airborne particles, wearing personal protective equipment (PPE), and maintaining clean facilities. The best way to avoid infection with COVID-19 would be for organizations to take safety measures that will help them reduce the chances of the spread of the disease.

Respirators provide another method for removing viruses from the air. They use cartridges with activated carbon to trap dust particles. The respirator is able to prevent particles like COVID-19 or any other pathogens from entering the body or infecting cells in the body. This prevents the infection from progressing into the tissues and spreading throughout organs.

A respirator is used to protect workers in hazardous environments, such as heavy industry. It is designed for use in situations where you will be working with harmful airborne contaminants, such as viruses and bacteria that can infect human bodies and cause disease. The respirator works by collecting and removing airborne particles before they can reach the lungs.

One of the greatest ways to prevent infection is by maintaining excellent ventilation and an air filtration system in your workplace. This would ensure that the air you breathe is purified and does not contain harmful airborne pathogens. This could be done either through the use of a filter or by using a filtration system such as what you would see in hospitals or other healthcare facilities. Filters such as these work to capture harmful particles and release clean air into the room.

United States Department of Homeland Security suggests using two medically acceptable methods for protection. The first method is the use of an N95 respirator, and the second method is by using a face mask with filters. These masks offer better protection than older style masks, such as the 2-piece surgeon's mask. These masks work on a daily basis, and they are very simple to use. These masks have been proven to be highly effective in preventing the spread of airborne pathogens.

The N95 respirators that are recommended work just like any other type of respirator and provide protection against COVID-19 and other airborne pathogens. The respirators are designed to fit most adults and they come in two styles. One of the styles is a tight-fitting suit and the other is a one-piece suit with a hood and gloves. These suits must be worn over a hospital gown or loose cloth attire to avoid skin exposure.

The most efficient way to deal with COVID-19 is to keep your hands clean. It is recommended that you wash your hands thoroughly with soap and warm running water for at least twenty seconds. This is done five times after each time you use the restroom. Wash with soap again after any exposure to bodily fluids or waste products, such as blood or feces. You can also use hand sanitizers that are designed to remove germs and bacteria from the skin. Be certain to always follow the directions on the label on the hand sanitizer, and remember that anything that is placed in your mouth can also be transferred to your hands.

Another way of preventing the spread of COVID-19 is by wearing gloves. Rubber or vinyl gloves are designed to provide maximum protection against pathogens. They should be worn whenever you enter a hospital, healthcare facility, or other places where airborne illnesses are known to exist.

Water filtration systems may also be used to prevent the spread of viruses and bacteria. These systems work by removing harmful particles from tap water, such as COVID-19, that can cause illness. They can be purchased at most stores and online retailers and they usually take around twenty minutes to install. They filter out harmful particles from the water as it travels through the filter and eventually delivers clean water back into the home.

You can also reduce the spread of COVID-19 by keeping your hands away from your mouth, nose, and eyes. This is something that you should remember to do at all times. Avoid touching these areas whenever possible, especially when you are in public or around other people. You can use hand sanitizer to remove germs from your hands after they have contacted these areas of the body.

In terms of prevention for businesses, the most important thing to do would be to use a good quality exhaust system. Equipment filters are also very important for companies that have certain machinery. Companies that are susceptible to COVID-19 infections should also ensure that their employees are properly educated about the dangers of the disease and provide them with sufficient training.

Another key factor for businesses is to ensure that they are following the proper safety protocols. To ensure that workers are not infected, businesses should train them on how to use their respirators properly. Part of making sure that employees are using their respirators the right way includes having them fitted by a professional.

Generally speaking, when companies are using disinfectants in their environments, they should make sure that these are being used in an appropriate manner to prevent the spread of the disease.

Finally, many people can also prevent themselves from getting COVID-19 by avoiding extended time spent outside without a protective suit. This will help people prevent exposure to the disease, which can lead to exposure to COVID-19. Since outdoor workers are more likely to be exposed to the virus, it is important for them to ensure that they are using protective suits when outside.

CAUTIONS WHEN APPLYING NATURAL REMEDIES

The number of reported cases of COVID-19 seems to be growing by the day. In order to safeguard against this virus, it's important that you get vaccinated! But there are some precautions you must do while applying natural remedies for your vaccinations so that you can avoid any possible adverse effects.

If you have a family history of allergies or other sensitivities, please consult your physician before starting your treatment so that they can recommend the best course of action for you.

It's important to keep in mind that natural remedies are meant to serve as a complement to your regular treatment plan. While they are an extremely effective way of preventing the spread of COVID-19, you should still consult your physician regularly for any possible side effects or allergic reactions.

While taking supplements is quite safe, it's important to remember that many contain high levels of nutrients. Increased consumption can be toxic in nature if taken in over-excessive amounts.

Be very cautious when consuming megadose of vitamins and minerals. The body needs to be able to regulate nutrient intake, meaning that you should take it in moderation. It is fairly safe to take any supplement that contains zinc, however, if you are planning on taking more than 2-3 grams per day, you should seek the advice of your physician first.

While it's important to include whole foods in your diet as much as possible, it's also important to eat a well-balanced diet. Including foods rich in nutrients like fruits and vegetables will ensure that you are getting everything you need to maintain good health.

While it's best to seek the advice of your physician before taking any supplements, there are plenty of safe natural remedies out there that can be used to treat COVID-19. The most effective treat for COVID-19 is definitely the vaccination. Keep this in mind!

These are the three easy tips to help you treat COVID-19 naturally:

1. Take a daily bath or shower at least every other day. This will help stimulate your lymphatic system by flushing out toxins.
2. Breathe through your nose. Breathing through our mouth is one of the easiest ways to take in large amounts of germs, including COVID-19
3. Drink lots of water. Staying hydrated will help

optimize blood circulation, which is one of the best ways to flush germs away.

While COVID-19 is a virus that can be fatal to your health, it is definitely possible to treat it naturally. As long as you don't have severe allergies or other sensitivities, you should be able to coexist with this virus and treat it through natural means. Try to follow these simple tips and you should be able to handle your vaccinations with ease!

DISCLAIMER: This is for information and education purposes only and does not constitute as medical advice or as any kind of medical treatment. Please consult your physician for the right diagnosis and treatment before using anything mentioned herein.

EXERCISE AND NUTRITION TO PREVENT COVID-19

The more fit a person is then the stronger their immune system will be. There are a few different ways that a person can be more physically fit. Exercise and nutrition are two factors that can help keep a person healthy through keeping them in shape.

Exercise is so very important because it strengthens the heart and lungs, along with strengthening all of the muscles in the body. Stronger muscles mean less chance of injury from falls or disease. There are many ways to exercise, so everyone can find something that is right for them. The crucial thing is to work out regularly, even if the person only works out occasionally. Working out often helps the immune system to remain strong.

Nutrition is also important for keeping a person healthy. If a person eats well, they'll be able to maintain a healthy immune system and avoid dangerous diseases like COVID-19. A person can be extra healthy by eating a healthy diet. The more nutritious the food, the healthier the immune system will be and the less chance of disease. A balanced diet could help a person stay away from some health problems that might be preventable with proper nutrition. Individuals should always pay attention to what they eat. The immune system relies on things like vitamins and minerals that shouldn't be missed. The body needs certain nutrients to work correctly and stay healthy, and the immune system is no different. Food helps make up the cells of the body and keep them healthy, so if a person takes care of their immune system, they'll need to take care of their body as a whole by eating properly.

By having a healthy diet and maintaining a proper exercise regimen, people will be able to stay healthy and avoid long-term health problems. The immune system can protect against diseases, but it doesn't work alone. A person's lifestyle will also play a part in how healthy they are, so it's important to keep all of the parts working together in order to increase the chances of staying well. These things would allow the immune system to do its job without too many other contributions.

NATURAL STRATEGIES TO PROTECT AGAINST THE CORONAVIRUS

Applying natural strategies to protect your family against the coronavirus is a good way to lower the risks of contracting this illness. These are some easy steps to increase your family's protection.

I. Boost Vitamin C Levels

Vitamin C is known as an immune booster, and its effectiveness against the coronavirus is now being recognized by the scientific community. This essential nutrient helps your body develop white blood cells that help combat infections.

To boost the level of vitamin C in your system, eat foods that are rich in vitamin C like citrus fruits, broccoli, red peppers and strawberries. You may also choose to take supplements to help support your body's immunity to this virus.

II. Avoid processed foods

Processed foods are made in ways that strip them of their natural substances, making them devoid of vitamins and minerals. Many companies add ingredients to processed foods that can be toxic to your body, so opt for organic whole foods when possible. This will help you have the energy you need to fight off infections.

III. Boost Your Vitamin D Levels

Vitamin D is a very crucial part of your immunity as it helps your immune system identify which substances are healthy and those that are not. When your vitamin D levels are low, your immune system functions poorly because it cannot identify substances that are harmful to your body. It is recommended that you have at least 15 minutes of direct sunlight without sunscreen daily to help boost this nutrient in your body.

IV. Exercise Regularly

Exercise makes your immune system stronger by increasing the production of white blood cells that support immunity. This is needed to fight infections like the coronavirus. Just make sure that you don't overdo it; too much exercise can actually weaken your immune system because it causes too many white blood cells to be called into action, leaving less available for other areas of your body.

V. Clean Up Your Environment

It is not just about getting rid of your garbage; you should also try to clean up the air that you breathe every day by making sure that your home is free from mold and dust. When people who have respiratory problems breathe in particles from dust, mold and other substances, they can get sick.

VI. Minimize Stress

Stress may cause your immune system to function poorly by increasing your body's production of stress-related hormones that interfere with normal functioning. A good way to get rid of stress is to get outside and walk briskly for at least 30 minutes every day, more preferably in the early morning or evening, when you are fresh from a good night's sleep.

VII. Reduce Your Alcohol Intake

Alcohol can suppress your immune system by increasing the production of stress-related hormones that interfere with normal functioning. An occasional drink is good, but if you have been drinking regularly, it may be a good idea to cut back or stop altogether until this illness is a thing of the past.

VIII. Get Plenty of Sleep

Getting enough sleep every night helps your immune system work its best by boosting your body's production of white blood cells which support immunity and fight off infection. If you don't get enough sleep, you may not be able to fight off infections as well, which is why the CDC recommends that adults get seven to eight hours of sleep each night.

IX. Practice Proper Hand Hygiene

Health experts are now recommending that you wash your hands frequently with soap and warm water. This helps prevent the spread of infection. When you don't have some time to wash your hands, make sure that you use hand sanitizer when necessary to keep germs away.

X. Eat More Fruits and Veggies

To fight infections, it is essential that you play an active role in protecting yourself by consuming plenty of fruits and vegetables each day. While you are at it, make sure that you avoid processed foods.

XI. Do Not Share Personal Items

This includes things like towels, sheets, razors, cutlery and straws. This is not just to protect yourself against getting sick but also to prevent further spread of the disease. When you are part of a family that is trying to avoid sharing common items with one another, it may be helpful to buy separate sets of personal items for each person in the family.

XII. Stay Away from Crowded and Unhygienic Places

When you and your family members are feeling well and can breathe easily, options open up to you. Things like having a meal at home or going to the park without other people around may be great ways to enjoy life as you battle against this illness.

12

TIPS ON HOW TO PREPARE FOR VACCINATION AGAINST COVID-19.

A set of pre-vaccination guidelines followed by all patients who are vaccinated with the COVID-19 vaccine are recommended. The recommendations include the following:

- Don't get other vaccines at the same time. Avoid having any other vaccines for 14 days after the first vaccination.
- Make sure that your doctor receives a complete medical history from you before you go to a vaccination center.

You must make some appointment with your doctor and make sure to fill out all necessary information about your health background and drug allergies on the Special Conditions Form (SCF).

- If you have any symptoms after the vaccination, tell your doctor. It is important to find out the exact duration of your symptoms after vaccination and map out a plan on how you can treat them.
- Following vaccinations, it is advised to eat fruits and vegetables rich in vitamin C so as to help strengthen your immune system.
- The patient should not have a history of anaphylaxis from any components contained within the vaccine. It is also recommended that patients with any medical conditions to speak to their doctors before being vaccinated.
- To be properly protected, it is important that you receive two doses of vaccine at least 21 days apart.
- Patients should be placed under observation for the first 24 hours after injection. This will ensure that an adverse reaction does not occur.

HOW DOES THE DOCTOR DECIDE WHICH VACCINATION TO USE?

When it comes to deciding which vaccine to use for any particular patient, the doctor will typically base their decision on a number of different factors:

1. Health Status

The current health status of the patient will be the primary consideration in the choice of vaccine because a weak or compromised immune system will not respond well to vaccination. In addition, a fully immunized patient who has been previously vaccinated is unlikely to benefit from another dose of the same vaccine.

2. Patient History

In some scenario, a patient may have been vaccinated in the past with a particular type of vaccine and the doctor will be more likely to choose a different type of vaccine for that patient.

3. Vaccine Availability

The current availability of vaccines will be a consideration when choosing which vaccination to use. This is especially true in the case of preventive vaccines, where supply is often much more limited than demand.

4. Past Vaccination

For some cases, a doctor might recommend that a patient receive another dose of the same vaccine because the last vaccination was effective or because it is important for that patient to have completed their vaccination schedule.

5. Travel History

Some vaccines are not recommended for people who are planning to travel to certain areas. In this case, the doctor may recommend changing the vaccination schedule so that it does not interfere with travel plans. The doctor may also advise against traveling to an area after completing vaccination in order to ensure maximal protection from the vaccine.

6. Side Effects

The side effects of a particular vaccination can vary from one person to another, and some people may choose to forgo the vaccine in favor of other types of vaccinations that do not have side effects.

7. Allergic Reactions

Some people develop allergic reactions to vaccinations, and these individuals should avoid certain vaccines.

8. Patient Expectations

The patient's expectations for the vaccination will be a factor in how the doctor chooses which vaccine to give. When a patient has some questions or concerns about the vaccination, the doctor may give that patient more information about the side effects and benefits of choosing that particular vaccination.

13

WHAT WILL BE THE POSSIBLE SIDE EFFECTS OF VACCINATION AGAINST COVID-19?

It is important to tell the doctor if you had any problems after receiving a vaccine in the past.

The doctor will also want to know your medical history, especially whether you suffer from any allergies.

Doctors will ask about the history of certain conditions, because these can make some vaccinations unsafe.

For example, if you have a weak immune system, or an underlying disease such as cancer, or a blood clotting disorder, then you will need to tell the doctor about these conditions.

The doctors will also ask about your pregnancy and whether you are planning to become pregnant.

By talking to your doctor before going away on holiday, you will be able to give them all the needed information so they could create a health-care plan for you.

Statistics show that the best time to receive vaccination is between one and three months before travel. But, when you do not have sufficient time, don't wait until the last minute to receive your vaccination. This can be dangerous if there is a risk of contacting a disease while travelling.

You should never disregard a vaccination or delay it for a month or more. Even if you have a mild adverse reaction, this could be a sign of a greater problem that you will not be aware of until it is too late. But, if you have a severe adverse reaction, you should speak with your doctor as quickly as possible, so the necessary precautions can be taken.

Very rare side effects

Allergic reactions are the rarest side effect of any vaccine.

An allergic reaction (hypersensitivity) is a serious problem, and is considered a medical emergency.

If you experience any symptoms after vaccination, such as swelling of the face or difficulty breathing, you should seek immediate medical help.

It is also crucial that you tell your doctor if you have a history of ***anaphylaxis*** – a severe form of allergy – because this will mean that vaccination is not safe for you.

Another rare side effect is a type of ***encephalitis*** that is associated with vaccination. This condition is known as "vaccine-induced encephalitis" and can be fatal. If you receive a vaccination and then develop symptoms such as confusion, seeing flashing lights, and changes in behavior, you should seek medical help immediately.

Between one and three per cent of people who take vaccines will experience a mild reaction such as stomach ache or pain at the injection site. These symptoms usually last for around 24 hours or so after receiving the vaccination.

Could I get the vaccine when I'm sick?

A mild illness would not affect the safety or effectiveness of a vaccine. However, you should wait until you are recovered from your illness before getting your vaccine to keep from spreading the illness. You should also avoid getting any vaccinations in the period immediately after leaving hospital and before your immune system has a chance for recovery.

To receive the full benefit of your vaccination, it is also important that you take the recommended shots on time, without delays. If you are delayed, your immune system may not be able to cope with all of the vaccine.

WHY ARE WE STILL ARGUING OVER FACE MASKS, 20 MONTHS INTO THE PANDEMIC?

A new study by a group of blood specialists has concluded that it is time to accept the evidence that disease control is best achieved through voluntary disinfection of infected people, rather than quarantine or forced isolation. A number of countries have been issuing face masks, banning public assemblies and restricting the movement of people out of sites where known cases of infection have occurred. But these actions have been resisted by some health workers, academics and others who argue that there is no such scientific evidence that they really work.

The study, which has been published in the British Medical Journal, also says that the widespread distribution of the vaccine to date has reduced the number of infection cases.

Since early October, when vaccines were made available in more than 80 countries, there have been more than five million doses administered and reports of confirmed cases have dropped by 85 per cent since late September. The study concludes that vaccine is the most effective means of controlling the spread of infection.

Though the mask-wearing can lessen the possibility of spreading the virus through the air, it doesn't guarantee total immunity from infection. The World Health Organization has emphasized that all people, including health workers, should wear a mask when they have been exposed to the virus.

14

WHY THE COVID-19 PANDEMIC HAS A MAJOR EFFECT TO OUR MENTAL HEALTH?

As countries introduce measures to restrict movement as part of efforts to reduce the number of people infected with COVID-19, more and more of us are making huge changes to our daily routines. Traveling, or limiting movement are common methods used to deal with the anxiety of being in quarantine with COVID-19.

Although these techniques can be useful for us during pandemic, this approach actually has the opposite effect.

Although it seems effective, the more distance we put between ourselves and COVID-19, the more we increase our sense of fear and isolation. This ever-present fear can reduce our ability to function normally.

In addition, not having enough information about COVID-19 can make us anxious as this will lead to a loss of control over our lives. In some cases, this anxiety could even lead to other psychological disorders such as Phobic Disorder.

For these reasons, we should avoid these approach but to turn our attention to another approach which is much more effective for improving mental health during the pandemic.

What can we do to avoid Mental Health problems?

The answer is exercise.

Recent research studies indicate that by walking or walking and cycling we can lower appetite and reduce stress in our body.

Exercise will also help improve our cognition and mood, thus improving our mental and physical health and well-being.
This approach is effective for us because it will give us a sense of control over our lives and environment around us.
Exercise will also improve our self-esteem and self-confidence since we can do something to protect

ourselves against this illness.
Exercise during the COVID-19 Pandemic is the best method to reduce stress, anxiety and other psychological disorders.
Exercise during the COVID-19 Pandemic will be our best way to improve health and wellbeing.
Exercises are easy to do, though it is important to make sure that we make use of the right equipment and the proper way to avoid injuries.
Exercise will also help us maintain a healthy diet, which is a key factor in maintaining a healthy body and mind.

The benefits of exercise in reducing mental stress and anxiety during the COVID-19 pandemic is most effective when we use movement through cognitive tasks.

Cognitive tasks can help us improve our focus and attention both in our life and in the work place.

Another way to help improve our mental health is through making ourselves happy. This can be done by using positive thinking. For example, by using the cognitive behavioral therapy method to eliminate negative thoughts and replace them with positive thoughts can be a very effective way to improve our mental health. Another approach is by reducing stress through meditation and yoga, this method usually takes a long time, but it is very good to use this method if we have a lot of time to spend for it.

Another method to practice positive thinking is by thinking about the things that are good for us, such as sports to improve our physical health or using our time wisely. This method can be very effective because it will make us think about the present life, which is much easier to do if we are in a better mood.

Another approach to reduce stress and anxiety during the COVID-19 pandemic is through Yoga. Yoga involves breathing techniques and physical exercises, which can also improve our mental health by increasing concentration and reducing negative thoughts.

Another way to improve our mental health is through the "Eat Smart" campaign. This campaign promoted healthy and balanced diets and can reduce obesity and depression. The Eat Smart Campaign also promotes cooking methods which will help us build a healthy social network since we can share our experiences on cooking with each other.

Although COVID-19 can affect people differently, as a whole it does not directly cause the death of the victims. However, COVID-19 does increase the risk of mental health problems such as depression, anxiety and fatigue which can increase the risk of suicide.

Even though COVID-19 can cause serious effects on our mental health, it is important to note that the most effective way to avoid risks of suicide is to talk about it with a doctor or a psychologist.

Suicide is an intentional act of causing one's own death.

Suicide is often motivated by extreme pain, usually physical pain but also psychological hurt.

Some people may believe that suicide helps to end mental suffering caused by illnesses. However, if the person who attempts suicide survives, he or she may be subject to enormous guilt and regret for ending their own lives, leading to Post-Traumatic Stress Disorder (PTSD).

If a person is already suicidal, and they do not immediately take the medication that would work to prevent suicide, they may continue to view themselves as disabled and will continue to seek out ways to end their own lives. They may also find it harder for them to receive effective treatment, such as psychotherapy.

Some people who have survived an attempted suicide will experience symptoms such as depression, anxiety, and guilt that can persist for months or years afterwards.

It has been found that COVID-19 victims who survive will be more prone to long-term symptoms of Post-Traumatic Stress Disorder (PTSD).

Depression is an illness affecting the mind, body, and behavior. All people can feel depressed sometimes, but depression that continues for more than a few weeks is considered to be a depressive illness.

Depression may change the way you feel about yourself and your life. Depression may cause physical problems such as pain, headaches, stomach aches and upset stomachs. Routine events may seem too much for you to handle, and you could lose interest in activities you used to enjoy. Some people may also feel very sad and cry a lot, even when there is no real reason for this.

Depression can make a person feel that they have a problem which needs to be solved. They may believe that the world would be a better place if everyone felt how they do, and that everyone would be happy. This is an extreme case of depression, but people who suffer from this type of depression can find themselves feeling helpless and hopeless. Suicide is a way out of a life they see as impossible to deal with.

Sleep is a sign that the brain is working properly. Sleep prepares us for the next day and helps us to be healthy. However, sleep disorders are rising in the world because of the rising COVID-19 pandemic.

There are many sleep disorders that are caused by COVID-19 pandemic. This is because COVID-19 deteriorates the immune system, which affects the brain, and also causes inflammation of the central nervous system. Inflammation in brain tissue can cause sleep disorders.

THE PSYCHOLOGICAL EFFECTS OF COVID-19 RESPIRATORY ILLNESS

COVID-19 respiratory illness has many effects on the individual. The most debilitating effect is the fear of death.

The psychological effects of COVID-19 can be very disturbing for people, with significant emotional and physical impacts on their lives. Two important issues that arise include communicating with others about your disease, and dealing with treatment side effects.

There are many ways to communicate effectively about your disease with others, such as friends and family members, employers, and health care providers. One approach is to use "I" statements which come from a positive stance. "I would like..." or "I want...," can be effective strategies in discussing your illness and treatment options with others. An alternative method is to use the "we" approach: "We need to..." or "what we can do is...," are useful ways of speaking about your illness, symptoms, and treatment options. These approaches are effective in establishing a common goal for all involved in working together to manage symptoms and get well. It is very necessary to know that not everyone will react in the same way - some people may become too intrusive, while others may avoid talking about the disease altogether. It is necessary to be clear about your needs and expectations and communicate these clearly. Do not be afraid of what the other person may say; simply state, "I would like to hear about your concerns."

Another emotional response is fear of death. People with COVID-19 respiratory illness are often afraid that their bodies will stop working or they will die. Sometimes this can mean that you are not ready to talk with others, but the fear of death can also make it difficult for people who have severe respiratory illness to continue treatment. The fear of death can make it difficult for people to think clearly about their health issues, and can give rise to other major concerns. Therefore, learning from other people's experiences with the illness is useful in helping you move forward in dealing with your own clinical conditions.

Other major COVID-19 psychological problems include a sense of helplessness and a feeling that one is at the mercy of others or has "no control" over their condition. It is important to recognize that feelings like this arise from a belief that you "must" do something about your condition, and this is not necessarily accurate. Another difficulty can relate to cognitive dysfunction; many doctors and patients will bring specific concerns about the effects of respiratory illness on cognitive function into their relationship with the patient. Thus, it is important for both the patient and the doctor to learn how to communicate in a way that they each feel comfortable with, in order to find a middle ground where the best care possible can be provided.

Reducing stress can be important in coping with respiratory illness. Oftentimes, people dealing with respiratory illnesses are not able to do the things they used to do. It can be helpful to focus on what is "good" about you, especially when it comes to dealing with side effects. Some of the most well-known side effects are depression, anxiety, fatigue, and breathing problems. These are some of the major problems that are faced by patients who have respiratory illness.

COPING WITH STRESS DURING COVID-19 OUTBREAK

The people with whom I learned to cope best were those who did so during the period of the COVID-19 pandemic. Such coping is often difficult and requires conscious effort, especially in the face of widespread fear and uncertainty. For some, the stress was overwhelming. For others, it was manageable if they had good social support. Most people responded to such stressful situations by minimizing stressful experiences and focusing on what they could do to get through them successfully. This is a process called "coping.

Among my most significant coping strategies during the COVID-19 outbreak were related to my daily practices. These included regular attendance at activities, routines, rituals, and habits that served as sources of comfort and support in times of some uncertainty and stress. The list below contains some suggestions for people who face severe stress related to severe respiratory illness.

Be aware of cues that can trigger anxiety responses including your breathing rate or your heartbeat. Take notice of the people and activities that help you cope with stress and distress. Think about how you can do more of these things when you are upset. This may include getting involved in social activities, religious services, and exercise. You may be able to use your anxiety or fear as a signal to take action.

It is important to remember that staying positive and optimistic will help improve your health, while negative thinking will make it worse. Try to view your situation in the context of all the uncertainty related to COVID-19 - what you can still do, where you can get help, and how you can cope with the risk.

There are ways to cope with stress related to severe respiratory illness. All individuals faced with severe respiratory illness face some degree of stress, but many people with acute severe respiratory disease have particularly strong responses related to their condition.

To cope with the anxiety, anxiety management techniques are very useful. The effective use of cognitive behavioral therapy (CBT) has shown to reduce anxiety in patients with panic disorder. It may be used in conjunction with relaxation exercises. CBT is an important tool in treating respiratory-related anxiety, because it helps to identify and challenge irrational beliefs that contribute to respiratory symptoms. C-BT focuses on how thoughts about the illness influence the physical symptoms and fears associated with it, and how one's behaviors can reinforce or disrupt these beliefs. It emphasizes altering unhealthy beliefs and behaviors in order to feel less fearful and more in control of one's illness.

Coping with respiratory illness is difficult, so it is important to surround yourself with family, friends, and community members who are supportive of your treatment. Support groups are often helpful in connecting individuals with the same or similar conditions; this can be especially beneficial when there is no cure or when the cause of the disease is uncertain. Our family and friends can be a great source of encouragement and acceptance, and they can provide emotional support to the patient.

Communication is essential in the treatment of respiratory disease. Being able to talk with someone you trust about things that are difficult is helpful in coping with respiratory illness. A therapist is a professional who can help people express their feelings and better understand themselves and their relationships. However, most people will not require the services of a therapist, and most psychologists agree that you do not need to go to a psychologist or psychiatrist to talk about your illness.

During respiratory illness, it is important to deal with difficult emotions in order to maintain positive coping skills. Anger, guilt, embarrassment, and anxiety are normal responses when dealing with such situations.

Feeling angry or guilty about lung disease or having to take control of your life, is common among many people with COVID-19 respiratory illness. Yet, anger and guilt can impair coping skills, undermine breathing and sleep patterns, and increase stress responses.

POTENTIAL IMPLICATIONS FOR THE INDIVIDUALS WITH SUBSTANCE USE DISORDERS

The people who use opioids at high doses medically or who have opioid use disorder (OUD) face separate challenges to their respiratory health. Increased opioid use and OUD are growing issues in the United States, including Oklahoma. Oklahoma the Department of Mental Health & Substance Abuse Services or (ODMHSAS) is dedicated to providing comprehensive, integrated, effective services that promote well-being for individuals with or at risk for an SUD.

The relationship between opioids and the respiratory system.

This section will review three important topics in connection with opioids and respiratory health:

- The effects of chronic opioid use on the

respiratory system in people with chronic pain, OUD, or both.
- The effects of acute opioid exposure in people who do not have an opioid use disorder.
- The impact of opioids on our respiratory system in overdose.

Opioids are often used to treat chronic pain and other symptoms of disease. Opioids may be used for more than one reason: they may be analgesics (pain relieving), and/or may be used as a combination analgesic and muscle relaxant (Ibogaine-MIMS). The term opioid is used in this section to refer to drugs that interact with the body's opioid receptors. This includes prescription opioids such as codeine, morphine, and oxycodone, and illicit opioids such as heroin.

The overall effects of chronic opioid use on respiratory health depend both on the medications used and the dose. Opioids affect the respiratory system at many levels: they modify breathing patterns by directly affecting parts of the brain stem that control breathing; they influence sleep patterns; and they reduce levels of carbon dioxide in the blood.

Since opioids work in the brainstem to slow breathing, their use not only puts the user at danger of life-threatening or fatal overdose, it might also cause a harmful decrease in oxygen in the blood (hypoxemia).

The chronic respiratory disease is known to increase overdose mortality risk among individuals taking opioids, and thus decreased lung capacity from COVID-19 could similarly endanger this population. Differences in the respiratory effects of opioids by route of administration (such as snorting, smoking, and injecting) partly reflect their differing absorption rates and subsequent release rates in the body.

Vaping, like smoking, can also harm lung health because of the harm caused by the inhalation of nicotine, marijuana, or other harmful chemicals. Furthermore, nicotine vaping may increase the risk of addiction. Inhalation of marijuana could cause lung tissue and airway inflammation, and could affect the lungs in a way similar to smoking cigarettes. Cigarettes greatly harms the cells of the lung and diminishes the ability to respond to infection. In this case if you've got a COVID-19 virus, it's possible that vaping can cause you to suppress your immune system and get sick more often or it may cause the virus to become more potent.

A history of methamphetamine use can also put people at risk. Methamphetamine, one of the more dangerous illegal drugs, closely resembles crystal meth. This particular drug may have a more profound effect on the respiratory system than other psychedelics. MDMA, LSD, mushrooms and psilocybin are also used as recreational drugs. Methamphetamine abuse is characterized by hyperactivity of the central nervous system, which can lead to heart disease and hypertension.

The respiratory effects of other drugs, acting at the same target site as opioids, are also discussed. For example, marijuana and cocaine both affect the nervous system and compromise breathing function. As for alcohol abuse, chronic low-to-moderate drinking has been associated with reduced lung function and increased respiratory symptoms like some shortness of breath and wheezing (the latter attributed to its effect on the airways). Marijuana also impairs lung function; smokers who inhale secondhand marijuana smoke may suffer increased risk of respiratory infections.

For the purposes of this section, it should be noted that "substance abuse" refers to problems related to the use of prohibited substances, while "substance dependence" is the more serious form of drug dependence. Problematic substance used or abuse can occur in all ages and socio-economic groups. Sometimes these disorders manifest themselves in the form of drug addiction, which is often accompanied by some other mental health problems like depression, anxiety and other mood disorders.

The effects of substance use disorders in a person with a chronic respiratory disease are not good. Substance-dependent individuals often have other health conditions and behavioral problems, such as psychiatric illness and physical disorders, which can also affect their respiratory health. Using multiple drugs or alcohol simultaneously can significantly increase the risk of respiratory arrest.

ATTITUDES TOWARD IMMUNIZATIONS

Many people do not get their vaccines for reasons such as feeling uncomfortable with needles, insufficient education regarding the risks and benefits of vaccines, and not understanding the science behind the diseases. So why do so many individuals still refuse to get their recommended vaccinations? Many people are hesitant to get immunized for no real reason. Some people feel that immunization is unsafe and may protect against diseases that generally aren't dangerous. They may not understand the clinical science behind the vaccine and why it works when administered to an individual. These people might not understand what a disease is capable of, along with how it can be prevented by getting a certain vaccine. In their case, they would rather take the risk of getting a certain disease than getting a vaccine.

Some people are against getting vaccines because they don't want to put anything into their bodies. They feel that immunizations are an invasion of the body's health, so they avoid getting them. These people tend to be more worried about the side effects than they are about the diseases that they supposedly prevent. They might also fear that vaccines can spread infections.

The vaccine protects the individual against disease, but not everyone has the same protection level. Some people only need a certain vaccine in order to remain healthy. Other people, however, might need a combination of vaccinations to ensure that they are strong enough to fight off the diseases that they are at risk for transmitting. If a person has a poor immune system due to another disease or condition, they might not get the same amount of protection against diseases through vaccines.

Some people feel that getting vaccinated is a personal decision that shouldn't be forced upon them. They feel as if they should have the right to make their own choices, and prefer not to take any other chances with their lives. If a person doesn't want to take a chance by taking a vaccine, then they should just rest assured that their decision is in no way affecting the public health. They might worry that the vaccine is not worth it if they personally don't feel like they need it. Others feel that the risk of taking a vaccine is worth it, despite their personal feelings.

Many people don't know about the diseases that are prevented by vaccines. People might not be aware that there are some deadly diseases that are taken care of through immunizations, such as COVID-19. Not everyone knows how important vaccines are in protecting the public against deadly diseases. The information isn't always presented in a clear way, though. There are many myths about immunizations circulating around the world, which do little to prevent further spread of misinformation. The only way the things would change is if there is more information about vaccines and better education about them.

15

LESSONS LEARNED

Each country has their own particular situation. Despite the similarities between countries, there are many differences that are important to take into account when preparing for the next pandemic. An effective plan for dealing with COVID-19 should be able to take these differences into account in order to have a more effective plan.

It is important to note that although the countries were affected by similar factors, they suffered different levels of damage. Some countries had less impact than others due to certain circumstances that were unique to them. Countries that had the highest level of COVID-19 infection suffered the most severe damage. Countries that were already suffering from economic problems, like Argentina and Mexico, were hit harder than other countries.

Even though all countries suffered damage in some way, there are many factors that were unique to each country. These factors include which sectors of society were hardest hit by COVID-19, the specific mode of transmission (airborne or droplet) and which countries received their supplies first, when it became possible to ship them internationally. Each country does not necessarily respond in the same way to similar events, which makes it all the more important to prepare an effective plan for dealing with COVID-19 and other possible future pandemics. It is very essential that countries be able to adapt their plans in order to account for any new information that might be gained through experience.

The main factor that caused countries to suffer varying levels of damage is how effectively they were able to handle the pandemic and its economic fallout.

THE ROLE OF MEDIA INFLUENCING PEOPLE TO GET VACCINATED

Vaccinations are important for children. They lowers the risk of catching communicable diseases, and protects them against serious illnesses. Vaccination is also an effective way to protect adults from these diseases. It appears like a no-brainer, but there are some people who are not vaccinated due to fear or misunderstanding about risks associated with vaccines. This is irresponsible since it puts other people at risk for not being able to get vaccinated themselves due to greater obstacles in getting immunity through natural means, such as disease outbreaks. Even though people would die from diseases, it is a larger tragedy if lots of people do not get vaccinated due to their fears. So it is important to acknowledge the challenges surrounding vaccine myths and also educate individuals on how vaccines work so that they can make informed decisions.

There are a lot of misconceptions about vaccines, mostly because they have been brought up in the news in a way that makes them seem scary. One of the challenges is that information about vaccines is often misconstrued and the media only represents people's perceptions instead of factual evidence. I think that more transparency is needed about vaccinations. Media literacy would help people to understand how messages are conveyed and the influence of such messages on their decisions and perceptions of important matters. The public would be better informed about issues if information was presented with a thorough understanding of how one perspective can affects what they see, hear or read. People would have an easier time communicating their concerns about vaccines without fear of being misunderstood.

The media have a greater influence on people's lives than people think. It is a powerful tool that has the potential to spread messages and images that can impact how people perceive events, including vaccines. If information about vaccines were controlled by a reliable source, then the general public would benefit. That way, they would know that everything they read was based on facts.

State officials should take media coverage of vaccines seriously and work towards educating the public about accurate information regarding immunizations. Part of the problem is that the people who get vaccinated don't realize the extent to which the media can affect how they see it. It's important for them to have an open mind about all aspects of vaccination so that they can make educated decisions.

This pandemic has brought up many concerns about the safety of vaccines. Although individuals are naturally suspicious of vaccines, it is important to put things in perspective so people can have an accurate understanding of the risks involved. The media would be instrumental in ensuring that people understand risks associated with vaccines, which would allow them to feel comfortable about the process.

If you have ever seen the movie Contagion, it is about a pandemic. A group of people are trying to find a cure for this disease, but instead of finding the cause, they discover who is responsible for spreading it. It is later revealed that this outbreak was due to an experiment that failed. There are many unknowns about vaccines, but there are also many successful vaccines that are made to help lessen the likelihood of illness. It is necessary to stay prepared for an outbreak and to find a way to treat those who may be infected as soon as possible. State officials need to be more proactive when it comes to discouraging people from spreading myths about vaccines. Most people do not take the time to look into immunizations. They trust what they hear as truth without questioning sources or seeking additional information. If anything, they should look for a second opinion from an independent source that is reliable. Another concern is that people can get sick from vaccines. Although this is true in the rarest of cases, it doesn't mean that people should ignore the advantages of getting vaccinated. Some myths about vaccines are easy to debunk by seeking factual information, but some are more difficult since they are based on opinions shared on social media. The best way to find reliable information is to look at scientific evidence cited in published scientific studies, which usually deal with several data sets and complex mathematical models.

COVID-19 virus is new, but it cannot be spread by itself, the way people think. There is a need for vaccine development to prevent the spread of this virus. To what extent do you think the media should be responsible in informing people about this virus? Wouldn't it be better if they got involved in finding a cure, instead of creating more fear and scaring people off from getting vaccinated? They can benefit by spreading awareness and increasing communication and understanding between experts and non-experts, including the general public. I don't think it's fair to force people to immunize themselves when they don't understand how vaccines work. Vaccination is a great way to protect oneself from the common diseases. It's better to have less people getting sick. We just have to find the cure so that this pandemic does not come back. That would be the best situation in order to prevent many people from being infected.

HOW WE END THE PANDEMIC

We need to accelerate development and testing of a universal vaccine. We also need to ensure that we have responsive surveillance networks in place, pathways for admission and admission control, and the ability to track contacts rapidly.

But our proposals don't end there. In order for us to truly eradicate this pandemic, we must continue to work with communities on promoting safe practices such as hand washing with soap at every opportunity. We must also ensure that health workers across the globe are trained in safe infection prevention and control measures. We must support countries to strengthen their public health capacities by providing resources, training, expertise and tools so that they can effectively prevent, detect and respond to outbreaks of infectious diseases.

We cannot stand by while this pandemic causes untold numbers of deaths. We must to do all that we can to stop this pandemic now.

We need to continue to engage communities in improving healthcare access. When we do work with communities, we must remain aware of the complex and unique environments in which they work. This means listening to the stories of those most affected and engaging with them as individuals and as members of their community. We have to continue to work with communities to develop safe practices that will help prevent future outbreaks.

As a responsible individual, you can take steps to protect yourself and your family. You can do this by learning about the disease, preparing yourself and be vaccinated.

We cannot stop this pandemic alone. We need to work with communities and government to support efforts to strengthen our public health responses, help us overcome the obstacles we face, and find new ways that will allow us to effectively detect and respond to outbreaks of COVID-19 virus.

We have to continue to work with communities to develop safe practices that will help prevent future outbreaks. Maybe the important thing you can do is promote awareness of the disease and its implications in your family, friends, and to others, so that they are all prepared for this pandemic.

16

INFECTION CONTROL IN THE HEALTH CARE SETTING

A critical component of the prevention and control of infection in the medical setting is contaminated surfaces. Patient-clothing, bedding, and environmental surfaces can be easily contaminated with pathogens that are often on the patient's skin or in their saliva. These pathogens can also be introduced on patient-clothing items or bedding that has been previously used by other patients. Further, air currents may carry pathogens from one patient to another in different settings (e.g., rooming/refectory or nursing home rooms).

The human body is a complicated machine. It's made up of millions of different cells, which all have a job to do. For example, the body has millions of white blood cells that protect the body from infection and disease.

These white blood cells take on infections and diseases, and they fight them by destroying them. In order for this to happen, the white blood cells need to interact with other groups of cells inside the body called macrophages, which are also important for fighting off infections and diseases. The macrophages and white blood cells stay healthy every day by getting the proper nutrients and oxygen, and they work together to keep the body healthy and strong.

The body's immune system is a complex system that defends against disease. There are many different parts of the immune system, including the skin, which helps people fight germs the right way. The skin also removes impurities from the body to make sure that it stays healthy. The skin also keeps the body safe from outside invaders like germs and bacteria. If bodies didn't use their skin to remove these impurities, they would be very susceptible to getting sick.

When people are sick, their immune systems can't work as well because they don't have any illnesses. The body's immune system helps keep people healthy by fighting off diseases and infections before they can even cause serious health problems. Keeping people healthy is important for everyone, not just for patients. This is why it's important for health care workers to keep the hospital, nursing homes and other medical settings clean and sanitary.

CLEANLINESS IN HEALTHCARE SETTINGS IS CRITICALLY IMPORTANT FOR INFECTION CONTROL

There are two types of germs: harmless and harmful. Harmful germs cause infections in humans, and they can make people very sick and possibly even kill them. It's important for health care workers to keep their hands clean so they don't spread harmful germs to patients. The health care workers must wash their hands with soap and water, and they should use sanitizers, such as alcohol gel, in between patients. They should also avoid touching things that touch the patient's skin or that have touched their skin. If doctors or nurses touch their faces and mouths while they're working, they might get sick and pass the germs along to patients and other people who come in contact with them.

The immune system controls germs and diseases in the body, but it's also an important part of disease prevention.

Health care workers often talk about infection control in their offices when they're trying to prevent staff members from getting sick or spreading germs to other people.

There are many different factors that affect how easily germs spread in the hospital and in nursing homes, such as how clean the environment is, how many patients there are and what kind of illnesses they have. Doctors, nurses and health care workers all need to know about how germs spread so they can do their best to keep patients and staff members healthy.

PRECAUTIONARY MEASURES IN ACCORDANCE WITH PANDEMIC PREPAREDNESS GUIDELINES

Preparedness has many definitions of which the most common among public health officials is to ensure that proper steps are taken to anticipate, prevent, prepare for and respond to public health emergencies. The basic definition of preparedness comes from the CDC whose mission is "to protect the health and safety of the people...by preventing and controlling diseases, injuries, and disabilities".

While the science of preparedness has been around for a few decades, it has been expanded recently to incorporate more specific procedures that may be considered part of a "contingency plan". Nowadays, there are clear policies and procedures for pandemic preparedness and response. In the U.S., federal officials have created a system of pandemic response based on push and pull systems. Push involves contacting and educating the public about how to prepare for a pandemic and pull involves urging the government to take certain actions. The push and pull systems are both active, and specific actions can be taken by either system.

Many countries like the U.S., Canada, China, and Australia have taken steps to ensure that preparedness planning is part of their overall public health emergency response strategies. These strategies include the ability to detect and respond to a pandemic virus and monitor the spread of infection (to prevent an epidemic) and/or to provide assistance for an outbreak (in the case of a localized outbreak). For example, the U.S. has developed the National Strategy for Pandemic Influenza Risk Communication which describes how risk communication can be used to respond to public concerns.

There are currently plans to curb the threat of disease using both risk-mitigation and risk-reduction strategies; however, many of these plans are focused on quick, immediate measures. These measures can also lead to restrictions on movement, invasion of privacy, or other actions that are considered extreme. These measures could have a serious effect on the ability to treat patients. We propose the following recommendations to strengthen pandemic preparedness in Canada:

Recommendations for medical countermeasures

There are so many potential complications associated with the use of medical countermeasures against COVID-19 Virus. Virus often leads to increased infection rates in nearby susceptible animals which may be forced into contact with human beings. While the risk of person-to-person transmission may be low, it is still possible. It is important to note that in order to be effective, medical countermeasures must prevent the spread of infection and also be useful for treatment. If used in isolation, they may not provide enough protection against an outbreak or have a significant impact on the human population. One benefit of medical countermeasures is that they may decrease the amount needed for treatment or help reduce the likelihood of a new outbreak due to a lack of natural immunity. Treatment may also be more successful if medical countermeasures are used.

The following measures can be used to strengthen medical countermeasure implementation:

1. To strengthen the implementation of medical

countermeasures, governments should increase funding for research. Some government funding can be used to test drugs or vaccines. Medical research can also determine the best ways to treat patients who have been infected, including the use of antivirals that may already exist.

2. To strengthen the implementation of medical countermeasures, health care workers should be trained to treat patients. Due to the risk of infection, medical personnel must be isolated from the patient population. However, if there is an outbreak, medical personnel can reduce overall risk if they are able to provide identification of the virus and communicate it to other members of the population. This system is also useful for identifying rare infections.
3. To strengthen the implementation of medical countermeasures, people should have access to medical information. This is useful for informing patients of various actions they can take to reduce the risk of infection if they are being considered for treatment or are in close contact with an infected individual.
4. To strengthen the implementation of medical countermeasures, people should be made aware

of how potential treatments may affect them. There are some drugs that are only partially effective on some strains of virus. It is important for doctors to know how many strains are affecting their patients. Without this information, doctors may prescribe the wrong treatment. People should be made aware of the potential effectiveness of treatments or medical countermeasures to prevent confusion.

Recommendations for public health officials

In order to strengthen the implementation of public health strategies, there are some steps that can be taken by public health officials:

1. To strengthen the implementation of public health strategies, a government agency should encourage a regular exchange of information between provincial and territorial governments and federal agencies. This will allow all levels to remain in compliance with legislation regarding pandemic planning. At the same time, provincial and territorial governments should collaborate with federal agencies to ensure plans are developed across all jurisdictions.
2. To strengthen the implementation of public health strategies, there should be established

procedures for reporting potential cases of infection to the appropriate authorities. This shall allow the system to work as intended if an outbreak occurs.

3. To strengthen the implementation of public health strategies, there should be standard operating guidelines for physicians and health care workers applicable to every jurisdiction. This will ensure that the information shared with the public is accurate and accessible.
4. To strengthen the implementation of public health strategies, there should be established procedures for testing and recording various contacts of an infected person. This will allow health care officials to be prepared for potential outbreaks and to provide information to people in need of treatment. This will also allow authorities to properly identify infected individuals and make travel restrictions more effective when necessary.

17

THE SUCCESSFUL PANDEMIC RESPONSE

One of the key components in a successful pandemic response is a well-functioning health-care system that will be able to deal with the increased demand for care. Another key component in a successful pandemic response is using science and technology to detect potential cases and begin treatment efforts before the spread of the virus becomes too widespread. The current model for dealing with infectious disease outbreaks does not allow for quick or accurate diagnosis because it relies on clinical judgment instead of laboratory tests. The current model is straightforward and simple, whereas a rapid and accurate genetic test results in higher efficiency. The new model will be able to accurately identify infected cases and track the movements of the infection more efficiently. This will allow for more effective use of medication, improved time management for treatment, and faster identification of potential carriers.

In order to deal with a pandemic, it is important to have a well-functioning health care system. In many cases, it is possible for people with COVID-19 to recover completely with no permanent harm. However, this is not always the case. Dead tissue cannot be used to determine if a patient is positive for the virus, so blood testing must be used in order to detect COVID-19 infection. Additionally, PCR can only detect the presence of virus in a sample which means that it is important to have a method of determining how active the virus is in an individual. The rapid surge of virus cannot be detected by conventional methods. This irregularity makes it difficult to conduct proper surveillance or provide early diagnosis.

A key mechanism in dealing with a pandemic is surveillance. Surveillance requires a means by which to detect all people who may have been infected. In order to effectively deal with the spread of the virus, it is important to identify carriers as soon as possible. The surveillance system should be able evenly cover all scenarios, from small outbreaks in remote areas to large-scale outbreaks in metropolitan areas. This will allow for an accurate depiction of the spread of the virus. Most importantly, it will allow health care workers to respond quickly and effectively in order to deal with the infection. The surveillance system should be able to track both methods of transmission, direct contact and airborne methods. It should also be capable of following all three types of carriers (symptomatic, asymptomatic and dead).

The COVID-19 vaccine is designed to be extremely effective in prevention of the virus. The vaccine relies on dead virus being bound to proteins that are injected into the patient's system. This will allow for rapid absorption into the body's tissues, but not into the general circulation. While this may offer some protection against infection, there is still a risk of "transmission chain effects" where a carrier passes the virus to another, non-immune person. The transmission chain effect is the capacity to pass the virus, but not suffer any significant consequences. The vaccine was designed in order to prevent this potential effect.

THE FUTURE OF COVID-19 RESEARCH

The global response to the discovery of COVID-19 has been encouraging in that it was swift and coordinated. While several countries have chosen to quarantine all patients with suspected COVID-19, this has not been the response in many other nations. Some nations have chosen to treat patients in private hospitals until it can be determined if infection is present or not. While there are currently no treatments for COVID-19, multiple research teams are working on methods of treatment. A few teams have focused on anti-viral medication, while others have focused on drug delivery.

The largest concern with COVID-19 is that it will mutate into a more aggressive strain of the virus, one that does not respond to current treatments. The current mutations indicate an increasing virulence of the disease, but will not necessarily allow for increased resistance to current treatments. However, there have been multiple cases where patients have recovered from infection due to natural or vaccinated immune response.

While cases of deviant disease are currently rare, they do pose a threat to the community at large. The most common cases of deviant disease involve carriers who have been infected with COVID-19, but not sickened by it. For the most part, this is considered a good thing as it allows people to be exposed to the virus and develop an immune system response without any noticeable side effects. However, many carriers are unaware that they are carriers until they begin to pass the infection on to others. This poses a threat because there is no way of tracking them until they infect others.

The future for COVID-19 research will involve continuing to assist the remaining carriers with survival and developing new treatments.

COVID-19 has been described as one of the most dangerous viruses known, for reasons including its potential to cause extreme damage once it is able to enter the body, its high mortality rate, and its ability to escape antiviral drugs. This has caused numerous countries to set up quarantine measures for people who have been exposed to prevent the virus from spreading. Going forward, public health officials are recommending "active surveillance" of everyone potentially exposed to COVID-19, including individuals who are considered to be at low risk. Such surveillance will involve monitoring for any signs of infection in both symptomatic and asymptomatic carriers, who might be unaware that they are carrying the virus.

MANAGING THE PANDEMIC

The government of the West had to take control of the situation and manage it in order to ensure that no serious economic damage was done. While many countries were able to stabilize and recover, there were still huge problems occurring in many other countries. Although the economy was relatively stable, the impact it had on social systems was devastating.

The most effective way to deal with the pandemic would be for countries to share information about COVID-19 and how to treat it. In order to do this, the World Health Organization had to create a global surveillance system that could track all cases of COVID-19 infections. Along with tracking the spread of the virus, it also needs to be able stabilize other national medical programs in order to ensure that they have proper supplies for dealing with future outbreaks. It was decided that countries with a high level of COVID-19 activity would receive priority when it came to obtaining medications and other supplies necessary for fighting off the virus. This system was put into place as soon as possible to prevent the spread of the virus from being able spread further.

The surveillance system has been very effective, especially when it comes to preventing countries from experiencing a deadly outbreak. In order to make this, the surveillance system must be capable of monitoring all kinds of carriers in order to discover new cases or previously unknown cases. The system must also be capable of monitoring all methods of transmission, including airborne methods. This will allow for quick response time when new cases are discovered. It also allows for quick response time when a new method of transmission is discovered. It also allows for early intervention in the event that there is a new strain of COVID-19 virus.

The surveillance system is not only useful in preventing deadly outbreaks, but it is also useful in allowing countries to plan for future outbreaks. The system will allow for effective planning by allowing countries to monitor the spread of the virus, and therefore predicting where it will spread and what methods of transmission will be most prominent. Countries that are planning for future outbreaks can prepare in advance with this information. This will also prevent unnecessary suffering, when knowledge of what will happen is already available.

Despite the existence of the surveillance system, it has not stopped numerous countries from suffering economic damage. A relatively small number of countries have begun to collapse, due to the economic fallout from the pandemic. This has caused widespread social problems in many countries that were not previously suffering these problems. It has also caused the rate of poverty and unemployment to increase across almost all sectors of society. The governments of many of these countries have failed to take proper action in dealing with the problems. Since they did not properly prepare for the pandemic and were unprepared to deal with the economic fallout, they were not able to stabilize their social systems and protect themselves from long term impacts.

While many countries had some success, there were plenty of countries that were unable to keep the virus from causing serious economic damage. While most of these countries have taken some actions to prevent worse damage and improve their economy, there is still a very long way to go. Many areas around the world are still highly effected by COVID-19 and will continue to be affected by it for years to come.

HOW DOES THE COVAX FACILITY WORK?

Governments and philanthropists have provided vaccine developers with significant funding to support and help mitigate the risks of product development. In general, governments fund the development of pharmaceutical products that they intend to sell, while philanthropists support the development of vaccines for diseases that they feel should be treated.

In both systems, product developers have been given a considerable degree of latitude in designing the clinical trials necessary to support human testing. In turn, this clinical trial experience has provided a level of confidence in their ability to find and keep a sufficient number of volunteers for further clinical development.

The reality is that vaccine clinical trials are costly and potentially dangerous. For example, in some cases, vaccines that are intended to protect health care workers against 'hot' pathogens, such as HIV or Hepatitis B, might require that volunteers be subjected to controlled exposure to these viruses. Vaccine developers have agreed on standards for human testing which are designed to mitigate the risks associated with this research. An example of the standards being used is summarized below:

Phase I

Phase I studies are designed to test basic safety and tolerability of a product in humans at controlled settings. During this phase, volunteers are administered a dose (or doses) of an investigational product under closely supervised conditions. The main objective of the Phase I study is to define the safety and tolerability of a product. Volunteers receive an investigational product under typical or normal daily routine clinical settings at daycare centers, schools, workplace settings and home... The typical duration (or length) of Phase I studies is typically 3-6 months... Results from a Phase I study may not be predictive of the clinical efficacy of a product. However, Phase I studies can provide valuable information about the safety and tolerability of investigational products in humans.

Phase II

Phase II studies are designed to confirm the safety and tolerability profiles already established during a Phase I trial. In this phase, volunteers are administered a dose (or doses) of an investigational product under carefully controlled conditions which replicate real-world settings where the product will be used. The primary purpose of a Phase II study is to provide additional information about the safety and tolerability of the product. It is hoped that these studies will give additional information to support the design of larger clinical trials (Phase III) or to support the approval (licensure) of an investigational product for use in human populations. Phase II studies can also be used to test the effectiveness/efficacy of products in specific target populations. The length of Phase II studies is typically 12-18 months... Results from a Phase II study may not be predictive of clinical efficacy. However, Phase II studies can provide valuable information about the safety and effectiveness in patients in particular target populations or conditions.

Phase III

Phase III studies are designed to determine the efficacy (effectiveness) and tolerability (tolerance) of investigational products for specific uses in human disease. These clinical trials are intended to support the approval (licensure) process. The length of Phase III trials is typically 6-12 months... Phase III studies are typically conducted in multiple centers (hospitals, clinics, etc.) over a wide geographical area. The design of these studies is intended to confirm the effects of an investigational product under real-world conditions by testing the safety and effectiveness of that product in a large number of human populations under routine medical conditions.

Phase III studies provide critical information about the effectiveness and safety of an investigational product, which is used to evaluate if a product should be approved for use by regulatory agencies... Phase III clinical trials, by their very nature, provide much more reliable information about the safety and effectiveness of a product.

So far, COVAX has raised over US$10 billion. These funds are paying for doses for the 92 most resource-limited economies. These doses will be administered to the most vulnerable of the population. In order to ensure that these vulnerable populations do not become ill from vaccine-derived diseases, a global surveillance system has been established. This surveillance system is a collaboration of governments, development partners and vaccine developers. COVAX expects more than 100 million doses to be delivered annually by 2040 – at which point it is expected that approximately 1 billion people will have been immunized against COVID-19.

18

THE RECOVERY FROM COVID-19 PANDEMIC

The COVID-19 pandemic has been characterizing global health crisis of this generation and reminds us of our global connection to each other. Even though the pandemic has been contained, there are still many people living with COVID-19 infection.

The COVID-19 pandemic was ultimately stopped by the speedy development of an effective vaccination that is being used on a global scale to always keep us safe from this devastating virus. The development of this new vaccine was an unfathomable task, but it was accomplished by the dedication of thousands of researchers around the globe.

Today, there is a global optimism for a better future as people recover from COVID-19 infection. The pandemic affected us all. But there are still many ways for us to improve our global health in the future.

When you look at the COVID-19 crisis in this day and age, it is difficult to imagine that it could have happened in a world. The lack of a fast acting treatment left us with no other option but to develop a vaccine against a virus we had barely any knowledge of. This was the challenge that the researchers working on this new type of vaccine were faced with. If it hadn't been for their diligent work in research, this pandemic may have never been stopped.

After almost two years, many people are still affected by COVID-19. The virus has left people with life-altering conditions, leaving them with both physical and mental problems. Those who have fallen ill to COVID-19 are still trying to pick up the pieces of their lives two years later. Many of these patients are receiving treatment, and many clinics and hospitals have been designated as free clinics where COVID-19 patients can seek care. These people should be treated with the same respect and dignity as anyone else.

There is a global movement to bring awareness to COVID-19 and the people it has affected. Organizations like the World Health Organization are working to gather data on COVID-19 patients in order to provide them with better care in the future. The virus has already taken enough from us, and we need to do whatever we can to help those people who have been left behind.

A part of our recovery from COVID-19 may be to support those still struggling with the after effects of this pandemic. We must continue to stand together as a global community, and support each other as much as possible.

There is much work that still have to be done in order to eradicate the threat of a future pandemic from spreading around the world. Many of the researchers behind the development of this new vaccine are moving on to different illnesses, but there is still so much to be done. The dangers of future pandemics are still looming, and we must continue work to protect ourselves for the future.

This COVID-19 pandemic has shown us that there is no other option but to be prepared for any type of global health crisis that may come our way. If we work together as a global community, this pandemic may not have been as devastating as it was. We can learn from our experience and ensure that nothing like it will ever happen again.

We can use the knowledge we gained from this pandemic to create a better and safer future. As we continue to move forward, we must remember those who have become sick and those also who have lost their lives as a result of COVID-19.

A FUTURE WITHOUT COVID-19

If you look back at the most defining moments of this generation, it is clear that the COVID-19 pandemic was one of them. This terrible illness affected everyone around the world, and has forced us to face our global connection. Although it will need some time before we can recover from this pandemic, there are things we can do to protect ourselves for future health crises.

One of the ways we can protect ourselves is by developing strategies to limit the spread of potential viruses. These strategies could be used in the future to prevent damage that is caused by unpredictable viruses like COVID-19.

We have to continue to work together as a global community to face these challenges. This pandemic taught us that our future depends on our willingness to be open, and it has forced us to realize that we are more connected than ever. This should give us enough motivation for taking action.

We have several work ahead of us to ensure a better global health for ourselves and our children. COVID-19 has been halted, but we must remain vigilant if we want to keep this from happening again. We have been already reminded that the only way we can ensure a safer world is through working together as a global community.

A NEW ERA OF GLOBAL COOPERATION

The COVID-19 pandemic has affected individuals all over the world, but its impact is still being felt every day. This pandemic reminds us of our global connection to each other in ways that we cannot imagine.

When you look back at this time, it is astonishing to see how much one virus has impacted our future. We all share with the same planet, and this is a reality that we need to remember. Although it may be hard, we must continue to move forward.

The COVID-19 epidemic has shown us that there are many factors that can contribute to the spread of an epidemic. While our medical advancements have led us to treat many of the world's illnesses, we must be prepared for how they can affect so many people.

With the development of different vaccine, we have learned that there are far more diseases that exist than we previously realized. This leaves us with much to be discovered, and many ways to move forward in ensuring better global health.

We must also use the knowledge we have gained from this pandemic to prevent it from ever happening again. There are organizations such as the World Health Organization working diligently to find out more about COVID-19, and how to treat patients affected by it. We must continue to aid these organizations in their efforts to better the future.

Global cooperation is necessary for our future, and we can see how much it has helped us in this fight against COVID-19. With the development of vaccines, we have much more knowledge than has previously been accessible. The technology that will be developed in the future will ensure that COVID-19 pandemics are less likely to occur, and allow us to move forward with a brighter future.

19

FREQUENTLY ASKED QUESTIONS (FAQS) ABOUT COVID-19

There are so many questions going around regarding the COVID-19 vaccine. To understand some of the commonly asked questions, we have compiled a list of frequently asked questions and answers below.

1) How Effective Are Masks And Do They Need To Cover My Nose?

Mask wearing is a very easy and effective way to reduce transmission and save lives. The masks that are most effective at filtering the small particles that contain the virus (like COVID-19) are masks that cover both the nose and mouth.

Masks alone are not enough to totally protect an individual from the virus, but they will play an important role in protecting high risk individuals like frontline health care workers. COVID-19 is a small particle containing virus that can lodge in the nose and mouth. When people are not wearing a mask, they may inhale some of these particles which can cause respiratory issues. The masks can also protect others from being spread by a sick person who lacks awareness or insight into their illness.

When integrated with other safety measures such as physical distancing and practicing a good hygiene, they are a very effective way with little to no interfering with the normal life.

2) Why Do Governments Benefit From Helping To Ensure Other Countries Access Vaccines?

For governments, there are various reasons why they may pursue the purchase of vaccines for use by all people through the WHO, UNICEF or similar organizations. Besides saving lives, these programs can have other positive effects for governments as well. Since many vaccines are produced by industry, the purchase of vaccines used around the world can help generate much needed foreign exchange revenues for governments. This also helps to allow countries to purchase more vaccines. These programs are not about profit maximization or exploitation of other countries, but rather are about saving lives and reducing suffering.

3) What Are Other Ways To Prevent Infections?

Avoiding close contact with infected persons is another way to reduce transmission of illnesses. This is why it is best that you maintain a physical distance of at least 1 meter from persons who are sick with COVID-19. Getting vaccinated is another way for us to prevent infection and increase ourselves and family's protection against this deadly virus.

4) How Can We Trust Vaccines That Have Been Developed So Fast?

Vaccines are developed thoroughly before they are used. Most of the time, vaccines go through decades of clinical trials, animal tests and observation before they are used on humans. In the case of COVID-19, this has been done quite quickly because this virus has evolved to be quite deadly and aggressive. Vaccines are developed by scientists and researchers who work through a strict process to ensure that the vaccine is safe and effective.

5) Is Regularly Washing My Hands Enough To Protect Me?

Washing your hands with soap and water is very important in preventing the spread of COVID-19. However, this is not enough to protect yourself or others. It may be necessary to wear a mask in some situations. And being vaccinated is another important step to reduce your risk of infection.

6) Do I Still Have to Worry about Infection Even Though I'm Fit and Healthy?

Most people don't think about infections until they get sick. Of course, there are other threats to health besides infections, but luckily the risk of getting sick with COVID-19 is low. However, if you are healthy and do get sick with COVID-19, you should see your doctor for safe and effective treatment.

7) Can I Get Vaccinated Against COVID-19 While I Am Currently Sick With COVID-19?

No, you cannot get vaccinated against COVID-19 while you are sick with COVID-19. The reason is because the vaccine may trigger symptoms of the illness and make you sicker. People with COVID-19 who have symptoms must wait to be vaccinated until they have fully recovered from their illness and have already met the criteria for discontinuing isolation; those people without symptoms must also wait until they meet the criteria before being vaccinated. This guidance also applies to individuals who get COVID-19 before getting their second dose of vaccine.

8) Is sanitizer or hand sanitizer a good way to prevent the spread of COVID-19?

Hand sanitizers or a similar product cannot replace washing with soap and water. These products do not kill all the germs on your hands and can leave behind a residue that can cause skin irritations. Sanitizers have been shown to be so very effective against some germs, including COVID-19, but these products are not as effective as washing your hands using soap and water.

9) Are Antibiotics effective in treating COVID-19?

Antibiotics treat infections caused by bacteria. COVID-19 is a virus, so antibiotics would not help protect against or treat COVID-19. Some patients with COVID-19 might also develop a bacterial infection, like pneumonia. In that case, a doctor may prescribe an antibiotic to treat the bacterial infection.

10) Are certain activities safer than others?

In general, outdoor visits and activities are safer than indoor activities, and smaller gatherings are safer than crowds. This is because viruses spread differently depending on the activity and setting. For example, people who attend crowded parties and gatherings may be exposed to many more viruses than those who stay at home. And those who travel internationally may also be exposed to many more viruses than those who stay in one country.

11) Why Would I Want To Get My COVID-19 Vaccines At A Placement Not Ascended By the WHO?

When it comes to vaccines, getting your vaccines approved by the WHO means that many countries will recognize these vaccines as effective. The WHO is a very powerful organization that is involved in the approval of many vaccines around the world. However, some countries opt out of using vaccine approved by the WHO or do not allow for their use because they have different requirements and not all vaccines meet those requirements.

12) What Is The Most Important Thing For Me To Know Against COVID-19?

COVID-19 is a very serious disease. The key to preventing infection is reducing contact with sick people. If you must be in close contact with others, such as health care workers and others, always cover your mouth and your nose with a mask. Keeping hygienic habits such as washing your hands can also help reduce the spread of this infection.

Get vaccinated. COVID-19 is serious and can be particularly severe in some cases. It is best to avoid getting infected with this disease, which is why it is recommended that all travelers get vaccinated against COVID-19 before travelling.

13) Are there different recommendations for cancer patients and caregivers?

Because cancer patients with COVID-19 may be very sick, they should avoid close contact with other people, especially pregnant women and infants. Some cancer patients may need to wear masks to protect others from their germs. It is important for caregivers to know that they can pass the COVID-19 virus on to their patient if they are not careful about their own health.

14) What if I've already gotten a COVID-19 vaccine?

If you have already been vaccinated with COVID-19, there is no reason for you to worry about the vaccine. The vaccine is completely safe and will not make you sicker or trigger your immune system to attack healthy tissue.

15) Can I get COVID-19 from a blood transfusion?

There is no evidence that the virus which causes COVID-19 could be transmitted through a blood transfusion based on the American Red Cross.

16) Do I still need to take precautions if I get the COVID-19 vaccine?

People who get vaccinated for COVID-19 are also advised to take some precautions. These include using a mask when close contact is unavoidable, not sharing eating or drinking utensils, and washing hands more frequently using soap and water. Vaccinated people should still take precautions against the flu which is very prevalent during the winter months.

17) What about dietary supplements or over-the-counter treatments?

There are no dietary supplements or over-the-counter products that have been proven to prevent COVID-19 infection. Some products have even been shown to make the disease worse, including some over-the-counter cold remedies and herbal supplements. It is best to avoid all non-prescription cold remedies because they may contain herbs that will make your symptoms worse.

18) Who is at risk for serious complications from COVID-19?

All people who have been diagnosed with COVID-19 should be closely monitored in a medical setting because they may develop a serious infection. The elderly and immune-compromised people are at a particularly high risk for complications from this disease.

19) Who Is Helping To Develop A Cure For COVID-19?

Researchers are working to develop antiviral drugs that can fight the COVID-19 virus, but it is too soon to know if these medications will prove effective in tests on people. There is also a very low probability that the virus will mutate into a form that can be treated with antiviral drugs. What we know is that there is currently no cure for COVID-19 and only a limited number of antiviral drugs.

20) What Kind Of Treatments Are There For COVID-19?

Unfortunately there is no cure for COVID-19 and most patients die if they do not seek immediate medical care. However, some patients who seek treatment early may respond well to antiviral medications and may be able to survive this disease.

CONCLUSION

It is wholeheartedly hoped that after reading this book, the reader can gain a better understanding of the current situation and expectations, for countries that have been affected by COVID-19. I hope that it encouraged you to continue with vaccinations, as a means to keep the virus from striking again.

The vaccine has been extremely effective against the virus. Millions have been vaccinated, and the virus has started to stabilize. As a result, many people have been freed from quarantine and restrictions imposed on their lives by the governments.

COVID-19 is no ordinary disease. It changed the way that people live, and changed the way that people think. In a sense, it changed the world as we now know it.

I personally believe that there is a chance for recovery from this crisis. The effort put into vaccinations has been enormous, and has been carried out by the governments of many countries, as well as those who have volunteered their time to help their fellow man. The world is not yet at peace. However, I am sure that it will be soon, with the help of new medicines on the horizon.

The view of the future differs from person to person. I still remember when COVID-19 was first introduced, and how everyone was on edge about its spread. At first, I thought that it would spread worldwide and lead to a second worldwide pandemic, which would probably kill millions if not billions of people.

Today things are different. In most countries, COVID-19 has been contained. In fact, it seems that there is a worldwide policy of containment. The governments of the world are doing their best to prevent COVID-19 from spreading. There are so many reasons why this is very necessary, but one that stands out is the fact that there are many more new vaccines on the way. These new vaccines could end up saving millions of lives, as well as halting the flow of COVID-19.

Hopefully, one day we could look back and laugh at all the problems we had to deal with in the past. It is because of COVID-19 that we are experiencing a global pandemic right now. Fortunately, this crisis has led to improvements in medical treatment and vaccines...

No one will deny that COVID-19 was a turning point in history. It brought about changes for the better, not only for the people who suffered from the virus, but also for humanity as a whole...

We can all be thankful because of what happened during this global pandemic. We are lucky to have made it through this crisis with our lives. The world is now at peace, and because of medical advancements, people can live to see another day...

I hope that this book has provided you with a lot of facts and facts that will provide you with insight into what is happening in the world, and I pray that you will continue to live well, and the best wishes for the future...

GLOSSARY

Alphacoronavirus- Alphacoronaviruses are members of the first of the four genera of coronaviruses. They are positive-sense, single-stranded RNA viruses that infect mammals, including humans. They have spherical virions with club-shaped surface projections formed by trimers of the spike protein, and a viral envelope.

Antibody- An antibody, also known as an immunoglobulin, is a large, Y-shaped protein used by the immune system to identify and neutralize foreign objects such as pathogenic bacteria and viruses. The antibody recognizes a unique molecule of the pathogen, called an antigen.

Antigen- In immunology, an antigen is a molecule or molecular structure that can bind to a specific antibody or T-cell receptor. The presence of antigens in the body may trigger an immune response. The term antigen originally referred to a substance that is an antibody generator.

Betacoronavirus- Betacoronavirus is one of four genera of coronaviruses. Member viruses are enveloped, positive-strand RNA viruses that infect mammals. The natural reservoir for betacoronaviruses are bats and rodents. Rodents are the reservoir for the subgenus Embecovirus, while bats are the reservoir for the other subgenera.

Cardiomyocytes- Cardiomyocytes are the cells responsible for generating contractile force in the intact heart.

Coagulopathy- is a condition in which the blood's ability to coagulate (form clots) is impaired. This condition can cause a tendency toward prolonged or excessive bleeding (bleeding diathesis), which may occur spontaneously or following an injury or medical and dental procedures.

Coronaviridae- a family of single-stranded RNA viruses that are surrounded by a lipoprotein envelope with large club-shaped projections and that infect birds and many mammals including humans but with each species of virus usually having a restricted range of hosts.

Deltacoronavirus- Deltacoronavirus is one of the four genera of coronaviruses. It is in the subfamily Orthocoronavirinae of the family Coronaviridae. They are enveloped, positive-sense, single-stranded RNA viruses. Deltacoronaviruses infect mostly birds and some mammals.

Diphtheria- is a serious infection caused by strains of bacteria called Corynebacterium diphtheriae that make toxin (poison). It can lead to difficulty breathing, heart failure, paralysis, and even death.

Gammacoronavirus- Gammacoronavirus is one of the four genera of coronaviruses. It is in the subfamily Orthocoronavirinae of the family Coronaviridae. They are enveloped, positive-sense, single-stranded RNA viruses of zoonotic origin. Coronaviruses infect both animals and humans.

Genome- In the fields of molecular biology and genetics, a genome is all genetic information of an organism. It consists of nucleotide sequences of DNA. The genome includes both the genes and the noncoding DNA, as well as mitochondrial DNA and chloroplast DNA. The study of the genome is called genomics.

Influenza- commonly known as "the flu", is an infectious disease caused by influenza viruses. Symptoms range from mild to severe and often include fever, runny nose, sore throat, muscle pain, headache, coughing, and fatigue. These symptoms typically begin 1–2 days and less typically 3-4 days after exposure to the virus and last for about 2–8 days.

Macrophages- are specialized cells involved in the detection, phagocytosis and destruction of bacteria and other harmful organisms. In addition, they can also present antigens to T cells and initiate inflammation by releasing molecules (known as cytokines) that activate other cells.

Methamphetamine- is a potent central nervous system stimulant that is mainly used as a recreational drug and less commonly as a second-line treatment for attention deficit hyperactivity disorder and obesity.

Opioid- Opioids are substances that act on opioid receptors to produce morphine-like effects. Medically they are primarily used for pain relief, including anesthesia.

Pathogen- In biology, a pathogen in the oldest and broadest sense, is any organism that can produce disease. A pathogen may also be referred to as an infectious agent, or simply a germ.

Ribosome- Ribosomes are macromolecular machines, found within all living cells that perform biological protein synthesis. Ribosomes link amino acids together in the order specified by the codons of messenger RNA molecules to form polypeptide chains.

Thimerosal- Thiomersal, or thimerosal, is an organomercury compound. This compound is a well-established antiseptic and antifungal agent.

BIBLIOGRAPHY

Coronavirus disease (COVID-19). (2021, November 23). World Health Organization. Retrieved November 27, 2021, from https://www.who.int/emergencies/diseases/novel-coronavirus-2019

Coronavirus disease (COVID-19) information centre. (2021). UNICEF. Retrieved November 5, 2021, from https://www.unicef.org/coronavirus/covid-19?gclid=CjwKCAiAqIKNBhAIEiwAu_ZLDuSOcho40a4ZOPR_BiHyCTMzyIFlfOPyLVEkYYlJxw0Rr_UaajUL1BoCpuwQAvD_BwE

Coronavirus Disease (COVID-19) Pandemic. (2021). PAHO. Retrieved November 21, 2021, from https://www.paho.org/en/topics/coronavirus-infections/coronavirus-disease-covid-19-pandemic

COVID-19 Vaccines and underlying medical conditions. (2021, November 5). Multnomah County. Retrieved November 15, 2021, from https://www.multco.us/novel-coronavirus-covid-19/covid-19-vaccines-and-underlying-medical-conditions

Fang, H. (2021, April 15). *COVID-19: The Impact on the Economy and Policy Responses—A Review*. Asian Development Bank. Retrieved October 20, 2021, from https://www.adb.org/publications/covid-19-impact-economy-policy-responses-review

Gavi, the Vaccine Alliance. (2021). Gavi. Retrieved November 20, 2021, from https://www.gavi.org/

NCBI - WWW Error Blocked Diagnostic. (2021). NCBI. Retrieved November 27, 2021, from https://www.ncbi.nlm.nih.gov/books/NBK554776/

Page not found | Our Better World. (2021). Our Better World. Retrieved November 20, 2021, from https://www.ourbetterworld.org/series/mental-health/blog/coping-covid-19

Saladino, V. (2020). *The Psychological and Social Impact of Covid-19: New Perspectives of Well-Being*. Frontiers. Retrieved November 27, 2021, from https://www.frontiersin.org/articles/10.3389/fpsyg.2020.577684/full

United Nations. (2021). *Coronavirus*. Retrieved October 20, 2021, from https://www.un.org/en/coronavirus

WiRED International—Medical Education Programs. (2021). WiRED International. Retrieved November 18, 2021, from https://www.wiredhealthresources.net/mod-series-coronavirus-infection-control-topics.html

www.ingramcontent.com/pod-product-compliance
Lightning Source LLC
Chambersburg PA
CBHW030904080526
44589CB00010B/143
9781739993047